SKULLS:
ART in BONE

First published and distributed by
viction workshop ltd.

viction:ary™

viction workshop ltd.
Unit C, 7/F, Seabright Plaza, 9-23 Shell Street,
North Point, Hong Kong SAR
Website: victionary.com
Email: we@victionary.com
@victionworkshop
@victionworkshop
Bē @victionary
@victionary
小红书 @Victionary Books

Edited and produced by viction workshop ltd.
Creative direction: Victor Cheung
Design: Hazan Yeung
Editorial: Ynes Filleul, YL Lim
Coordination: Jeanie Choy, Katherine Wong
Production: Bryan Leung
Typefaces: Claus by Zetafonts Type Foundry, APOC by
Blaze Type, Aeonik Fono by CoType Foundry

ISBN 978-988-70660-4-0
Printed and bound in China

Contents

Preface

There is something magnetic about the skull.

It is both relic and reminder: regarded after we are gone as the vessel that once held our thoughts and laughter, our dreams and fears. When we gaze upon it, we see not only the trace of death, but the quiet architecture of life – the shape that unites us all beneath the skin.

For centuries, artists have turned to the skull as a mirror of existence. It has been worn in devotion, carved into tombs, and raised aloft as an act of rebellion. From the vanitas still lifes of the seventeenth century to the bright defiance of punk culture, it has always been more than bone – it is a symbol of the human condition, stripped of ornament yet endlessly adorned through art.

In SKULLS: ART IN BONE, this enduring form finds new voices. Each artist here approaches it not as an ending, but as a beginning – a place from which imagination grows. Some see it as an echo of the sacred, others as a playground of the absurd. Together, their works reveal the skull's infinite capacity to contain humour, beauty, sorrow, and light.

Sophie Donaj (pp. 118–125) reflects that skulls "symbolise life's transience yet feel deeply familiar," and it is this familiarity that allows the artists in these pages to push the image into new terrain. In the gleaming geometry of Billelis's intricate creations (pp. 306–311), the skull gleams like a relic from a dream. Jim Skull's handwoven forms (pp. 346–349) breathe with ritual quietness, each strand of fibre binding the living and the lost. For Kate MacDowell (pp. 336–341), the skull becomes part of the natural world, a reminder that our bones, too, return to earth and become its story.

Some, like Jimi Biscuits (pp. 66–67, 94–97), find comedy in mortality, transforming the skull into a mischievous character from everyday objects. Others, such as Laurina Paperina (pp. 258–263) embrace the absurd – her off-the-wall creations colliding pop-culture icons with skeletal forms.

To look through these pages is to witness the skull's many lives: sculpted, painted, pixelated, and reimagined across cultures and media. It endures because it belongs to everyone. Beneath it, there is no race, no class, no border – only the memory of having lived. Alexander de Cadenet (pp. 190, 312–313) posits that the skull is "a forensic record of your unique identity," yet its anonymity is what grants it universality. Perhaps that is why artists keep returning to it: because within its emptiness lies an invitation – to fill it with meaning, to see ourselves reflected in its quiet grin.

SKULLS: ART IN BONE gathers these reflections like fragments of a single thought shared across time. In their hands, the skull ceases to be a memento mori and becomes a memento vitae – a reminder not of how life ends, but of how creation endures.

Facial

Inspired by the facial bones that shape our features and expressions, this section showcases projects with the skull as a dynamic canvas - the centrepiece from which creative ideas, graphic elements, and intricate illustrations radiate, flow, or burst outward to evoke energy, emotion, and character.

pp.9-108

(11)

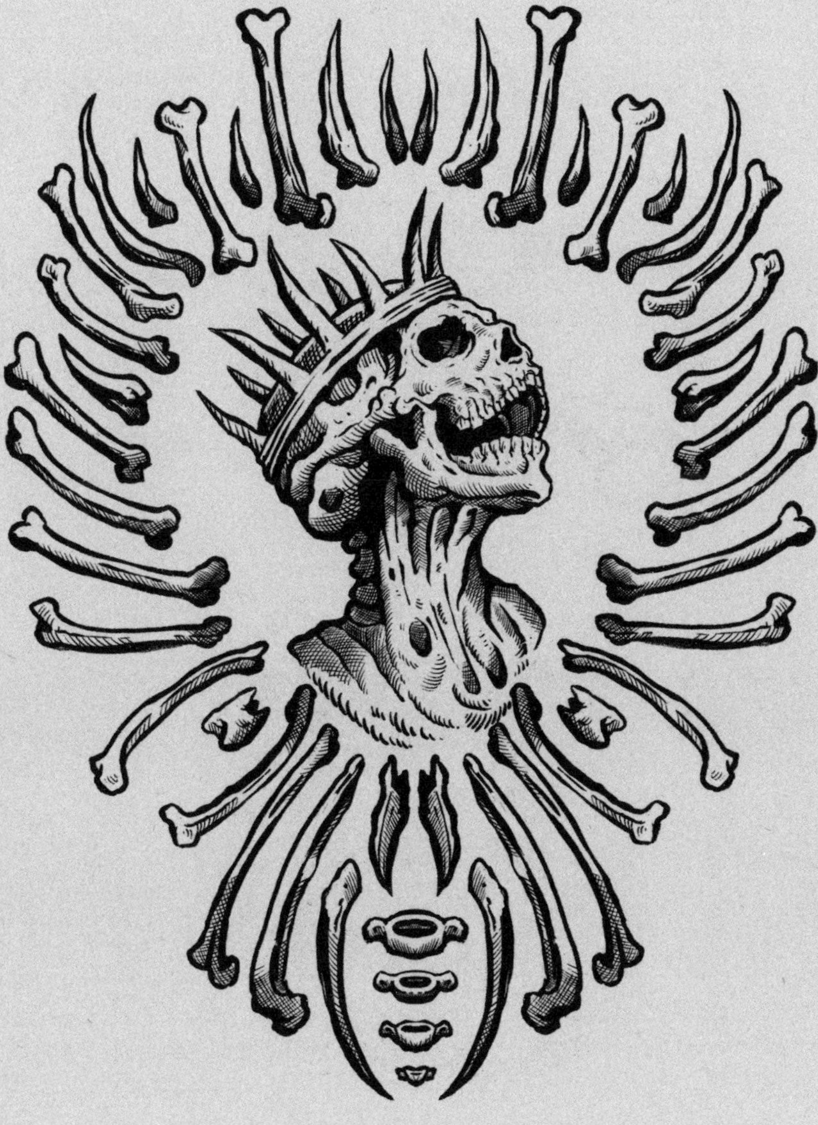

Bart.Woo

(12)

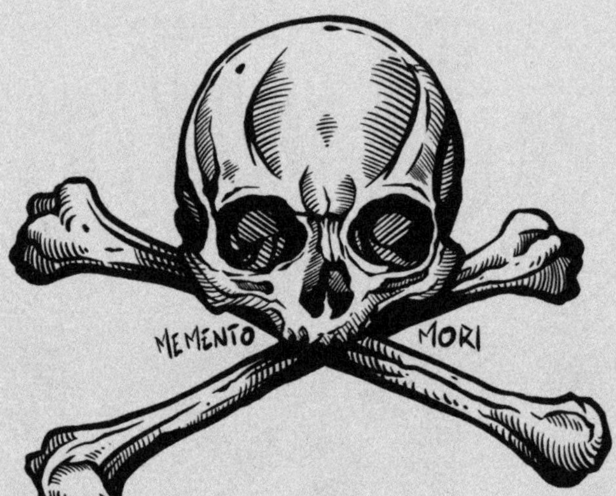

Bart.Woo

(13)

Bart.Woo

(14)

DEADLIFT

Bart.Woo

(15)

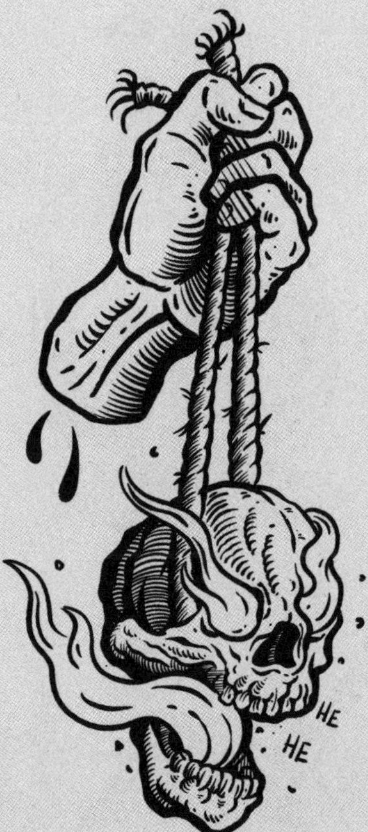

Bart.Woo

(16)

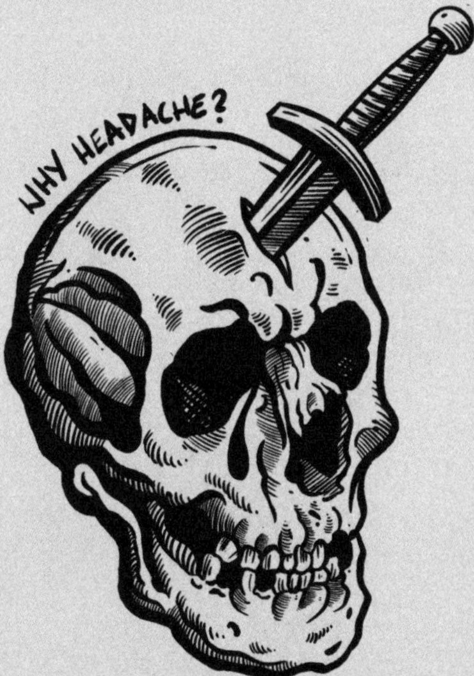

Bart.Woo

(17)

Bart.Woo

(18)

Bart.Woo

(19)

Bart.Woo

(20)

Pablo Dalas

(21)

Pablo Dalas

(22)

Pablo Dalas

(23)

Pablo Dalas

(24)

Pablo Dalas

(25)

Pablo Dalas

(26)

Pablo Dalas

(27)

Pablo Dalas

(28)

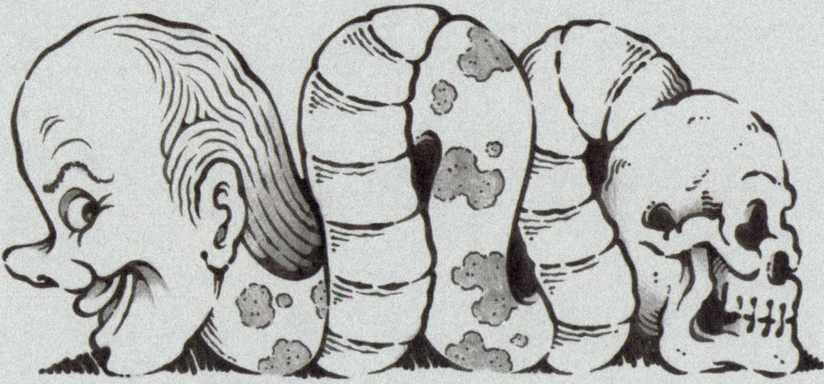

Pablo Dalas

(29)

Pablo Dalas

(30)

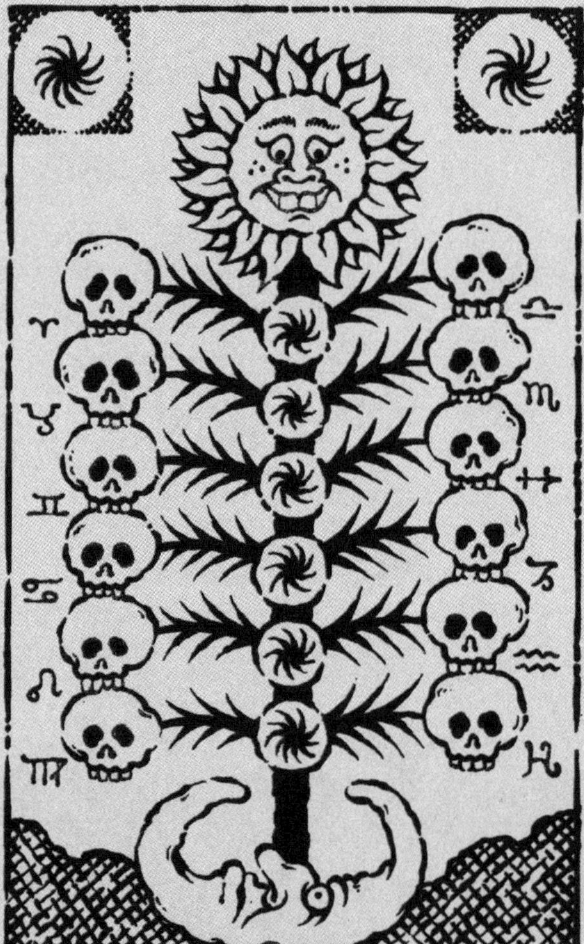

Pablo Dalas

(31)

Pablo Dalas

(32)

D.Vicente

(33)

D.Vicente

(34)

D.Vicente

(35)

D.Vicente

(36)

D.Vicente

(37)

KUSTOM...
RIDE
HARD
Dickies
SINCE
1922
D.Vicente
DICKIES
Clothing & Co.
CHOPPER

D.Vicente

(38)

D.Vicente

(39)

D.Vicente

(40)

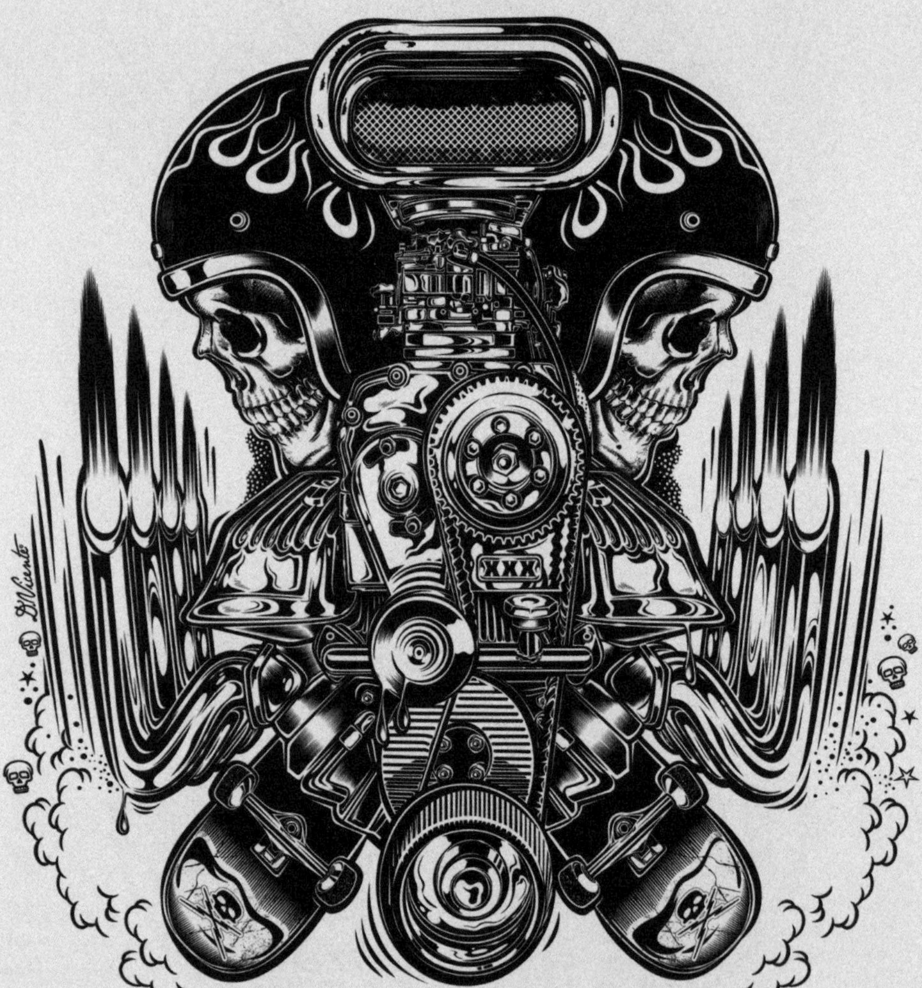

D.Vicente

(41)

D.Vicente

(42)

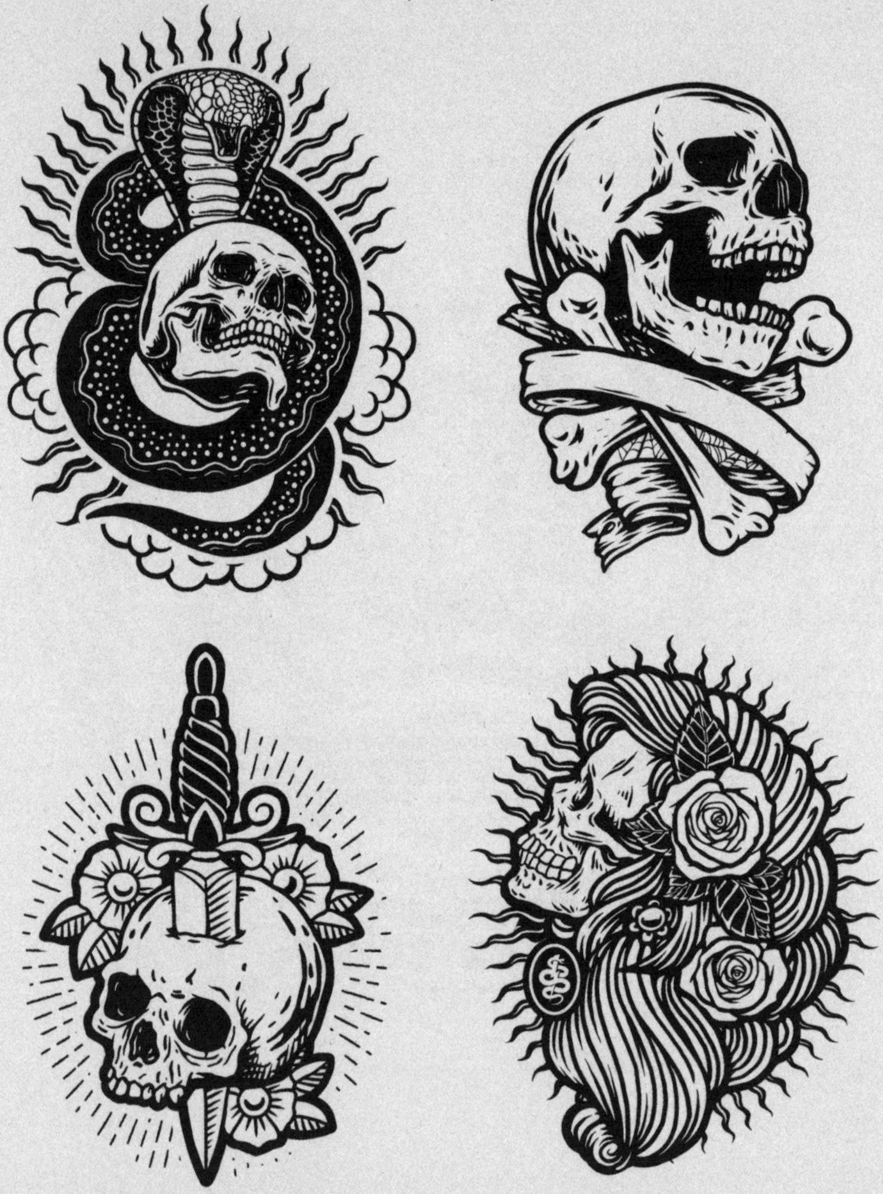

Paolo D. Geronimo

(43)

Paolo D. Geronimo

(44)

Paolo D. Geronimo

(45)

Paolo D. Geronimo

(46)

Paolo D. Geronimo

(47)

Paolo D. Geronimo

(48)

Paolo D. Geronimo

(49)

Paolo D. Geronimo

(50)

Paolo D. Geronimo

(51)

Paolo D. Geronimo

(52)

Paolo D. Geronimo

Paolo D. Geronimo

(54)

Paolo D. Geronimo

(55)

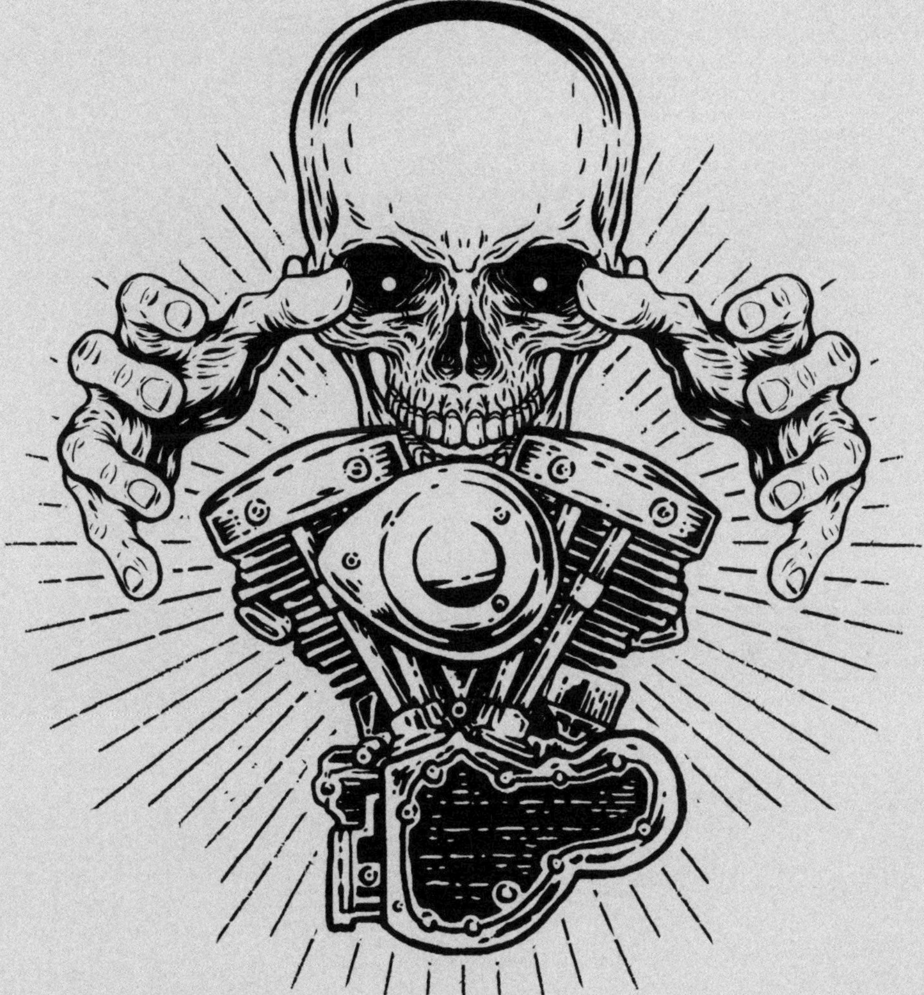

Paolo D. Geronimo

(56)

Paolo D. Geronimo

(57)

Paolo D. Geronimo

(58)

Betrayer Family

(59)

Betrayer Family

(60)

Betrayer Family

(61)

Betrayer Family

(62)

Betrayer Family

Betrayer Family

(64)

Betrayer Family

Betrayer Family

(66)

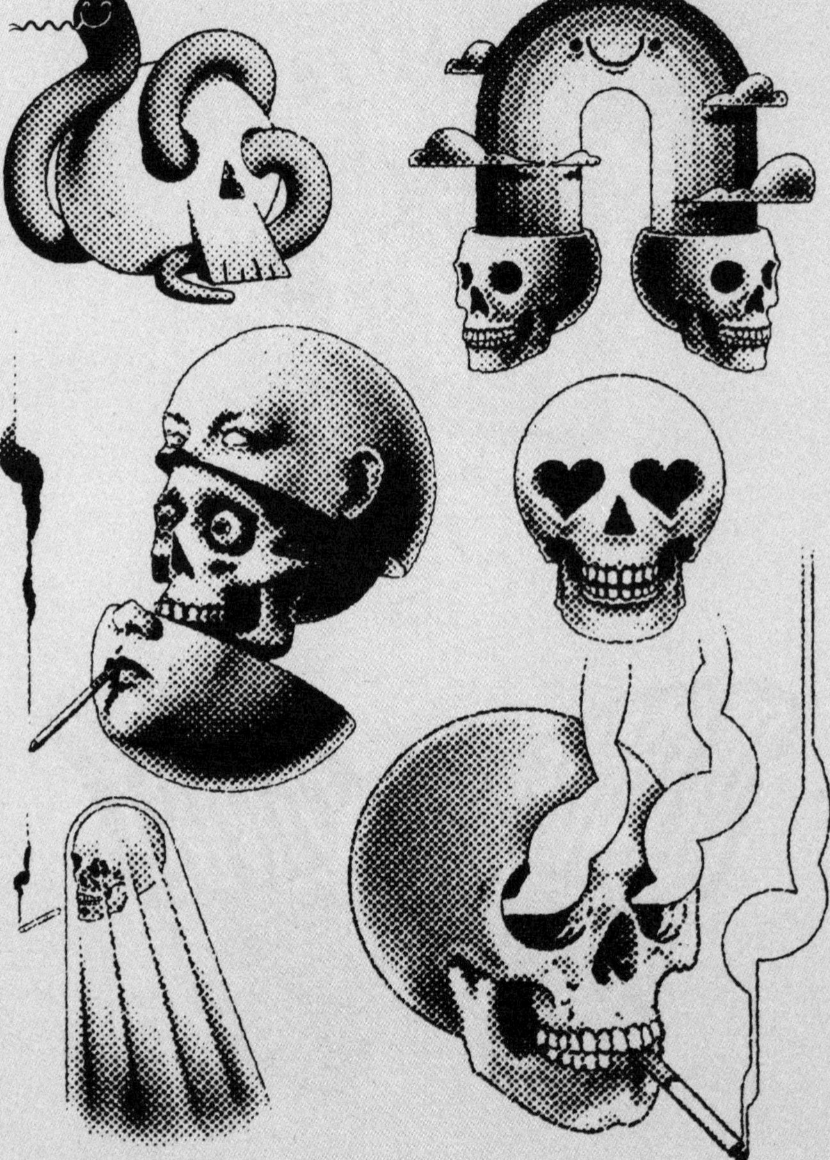

Jimi Biscuits

(67)

Jimi Biscuits

(68)

Vliegwerk Premium

(69)

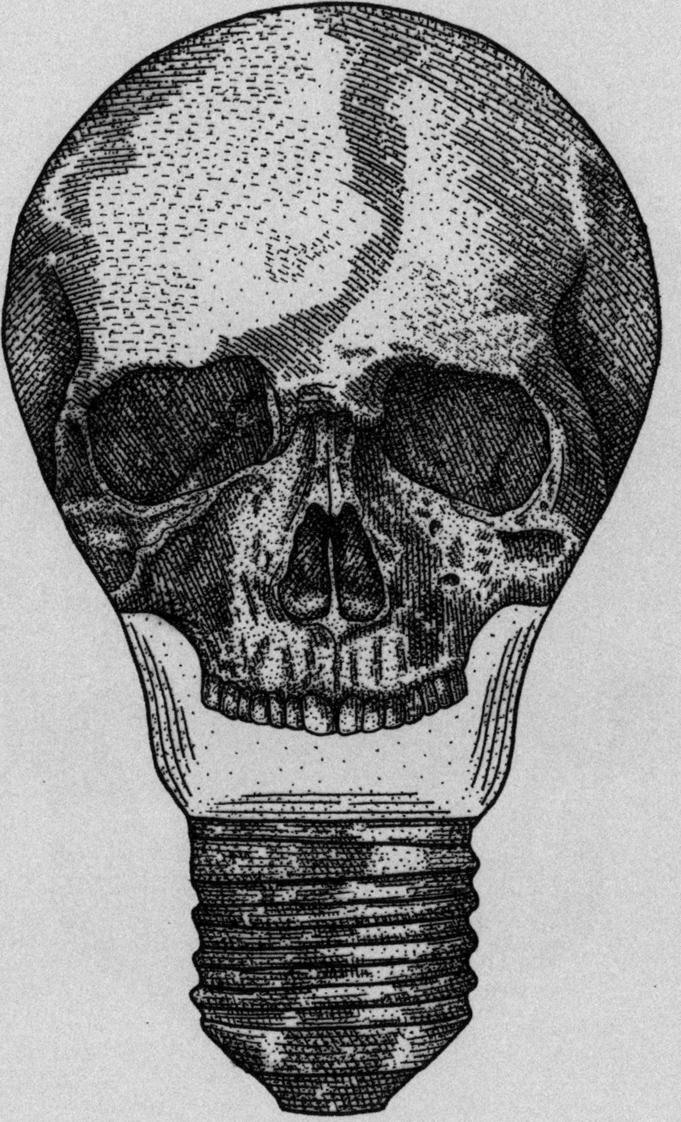

Vliegwerk Premium

(70)

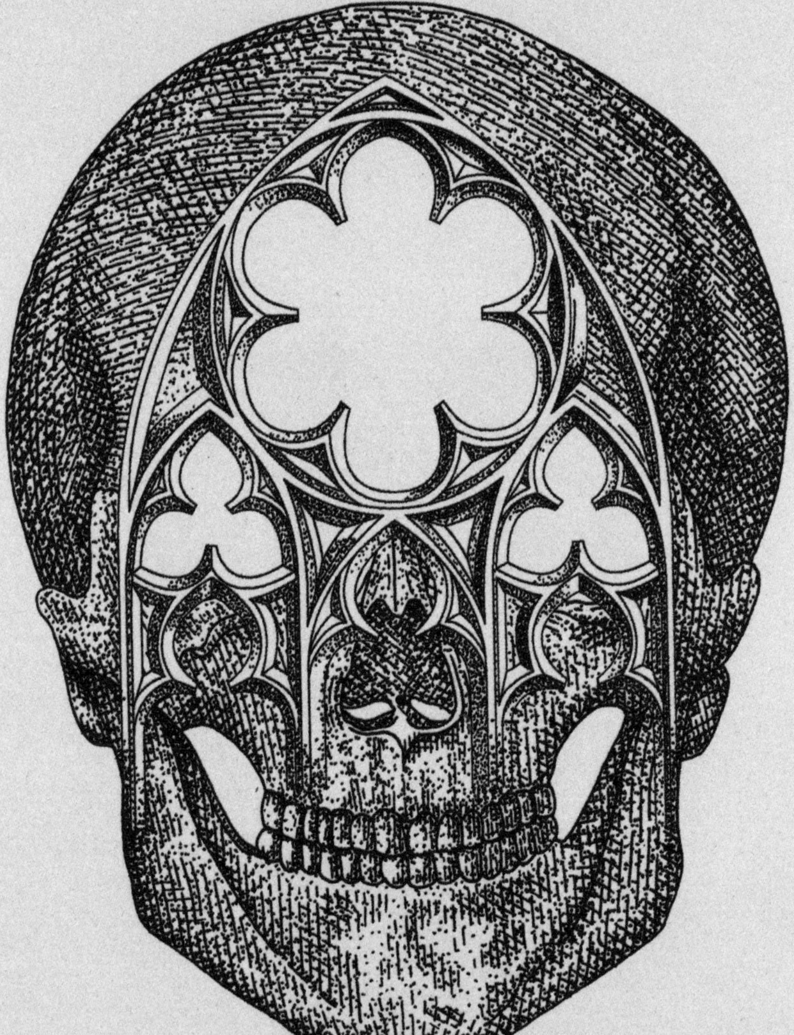

Vliegwerk Premium

(71)

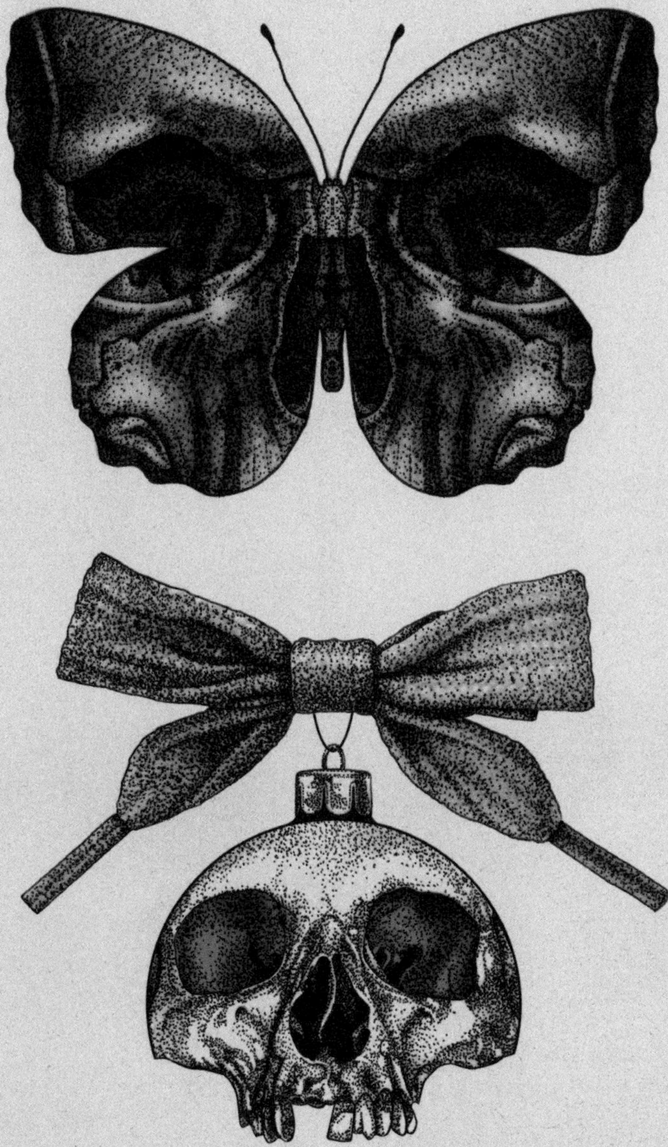

Vliegwerk Premium

(72)

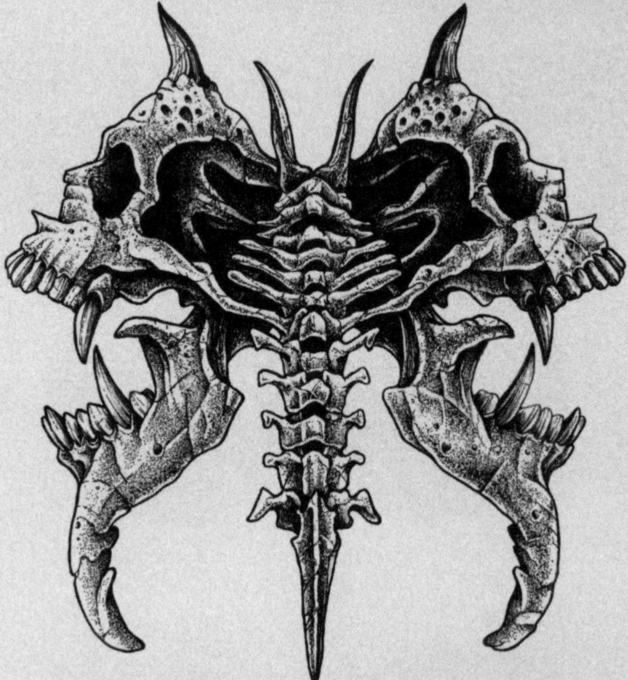

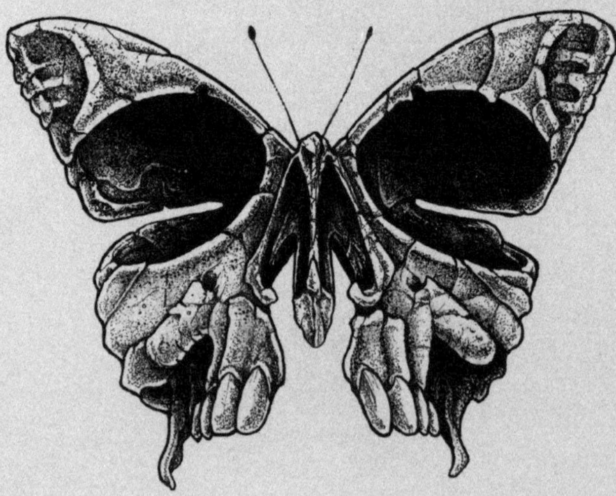

Sinpiggyhead

(73)

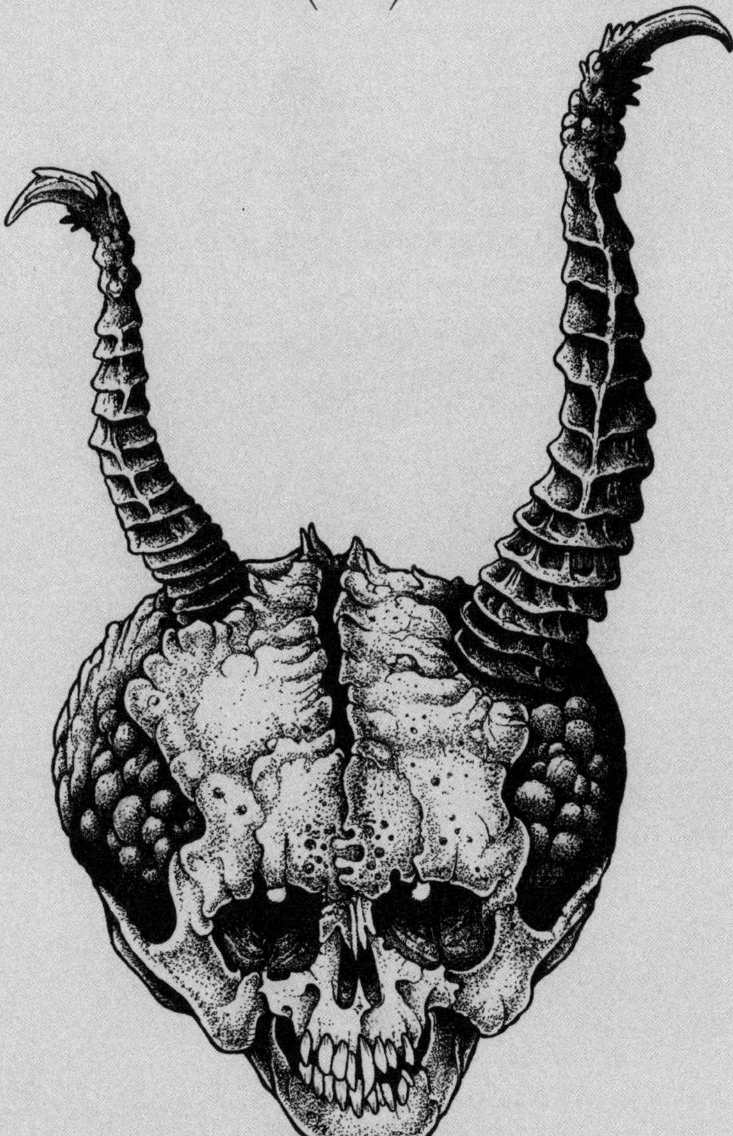

Sinpiggyhead

(74)

Sinpiggyhead

(75)

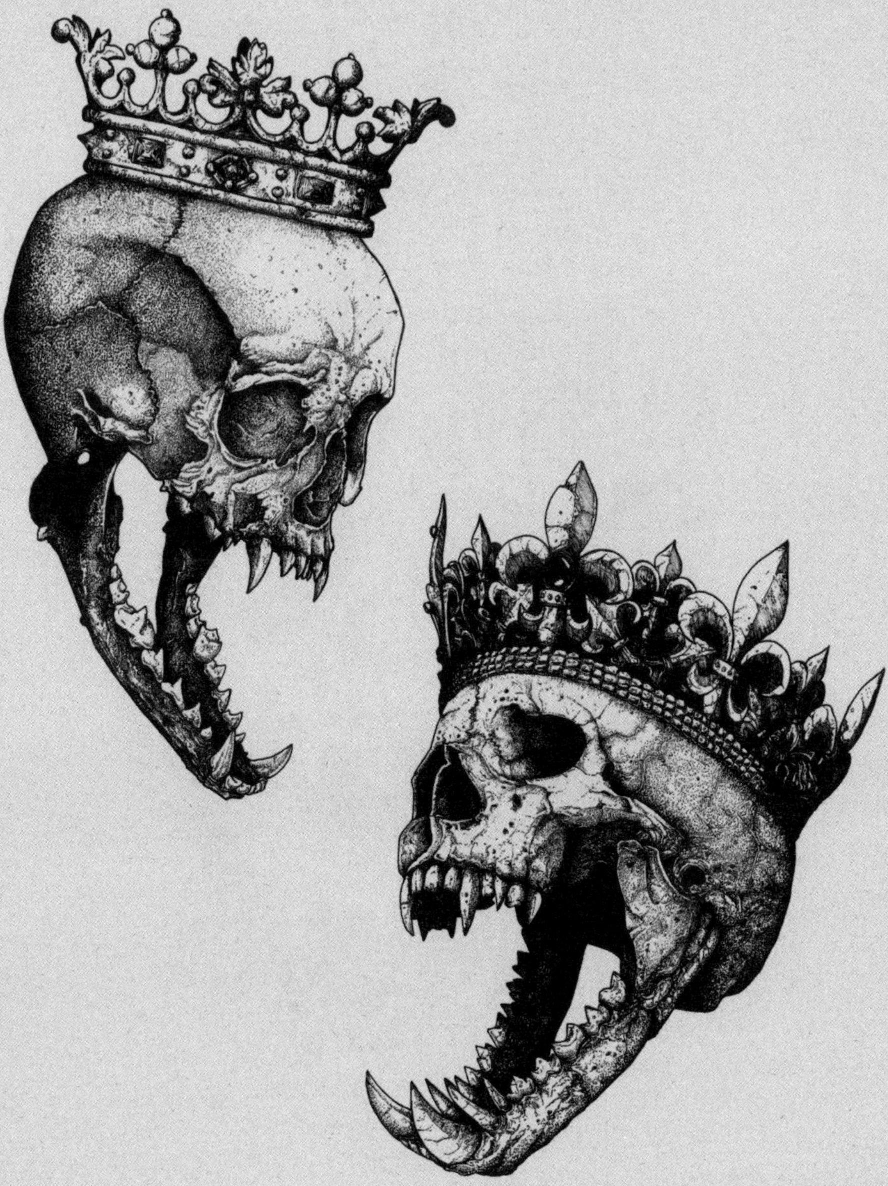

Sinpiggyhead

(76)

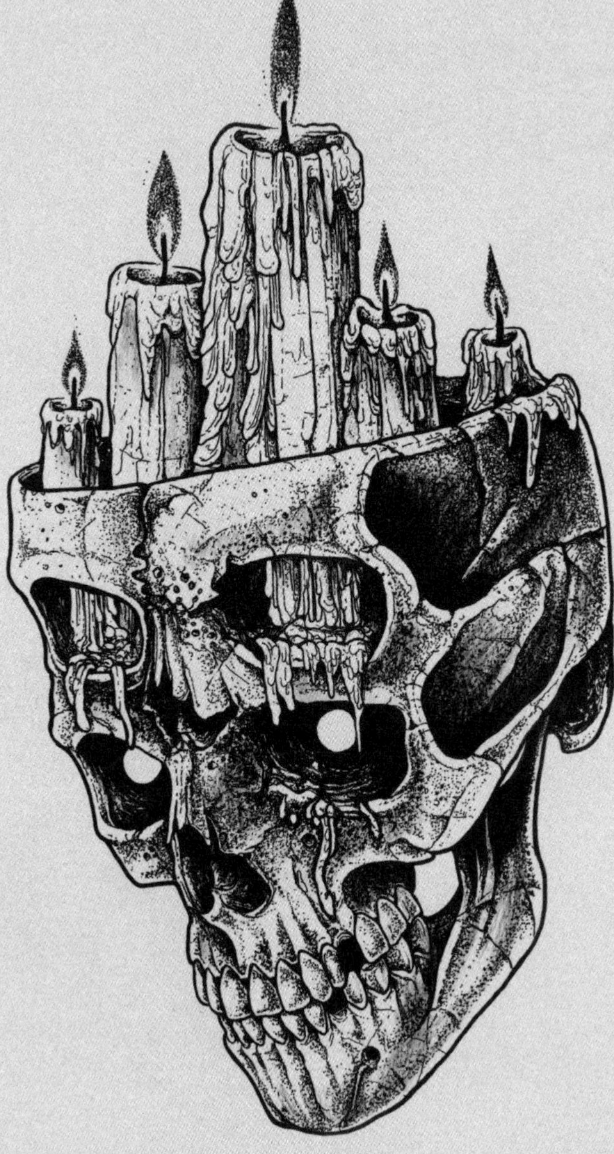

Sinpiggyhead

(77)

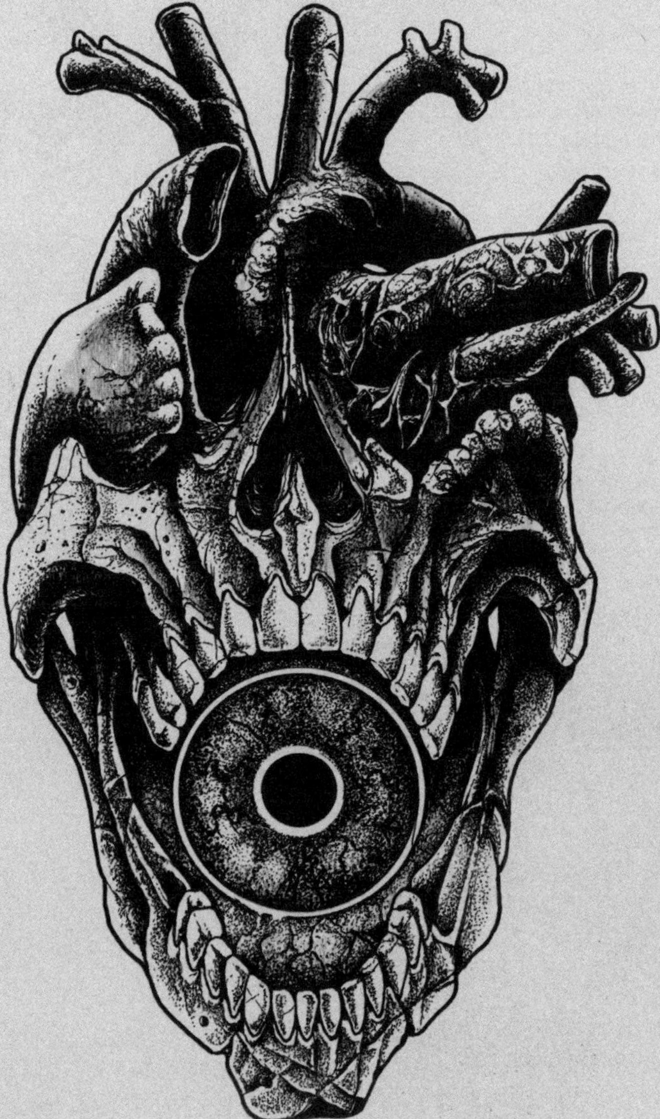

Sinpiggyhead

(78)

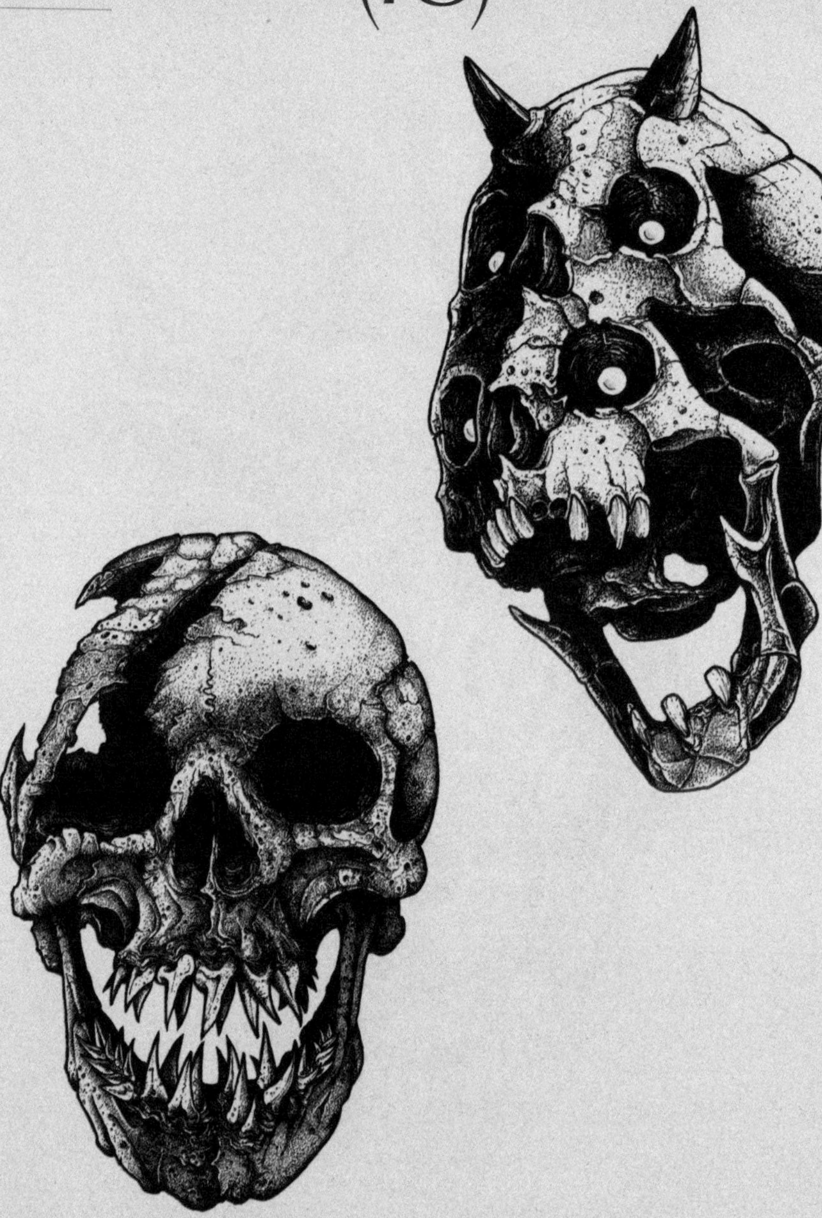

Sinpiggyhead

(79)

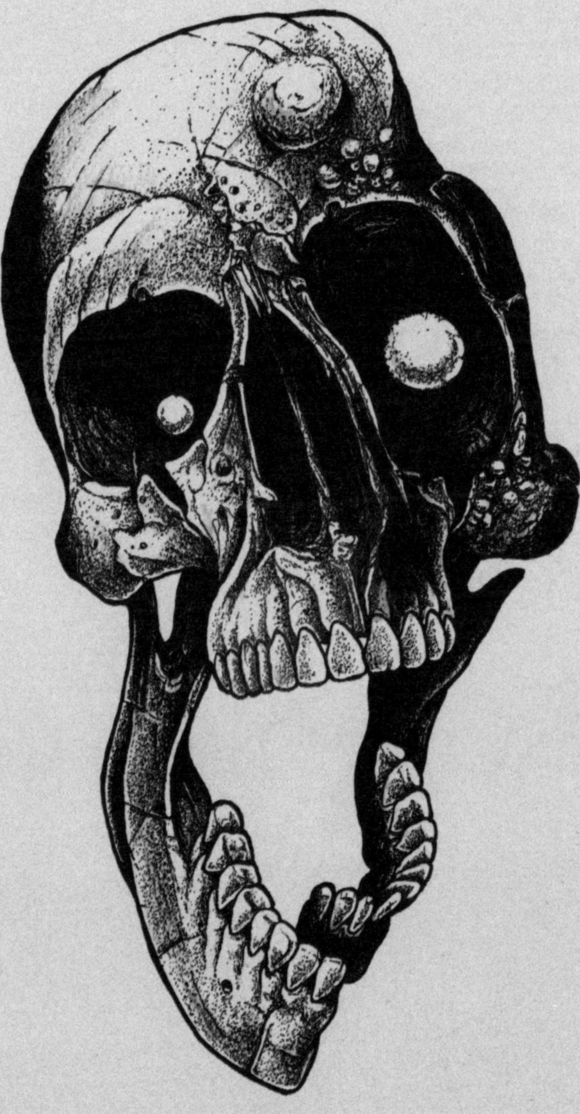

Sinpiggyhead

(80)

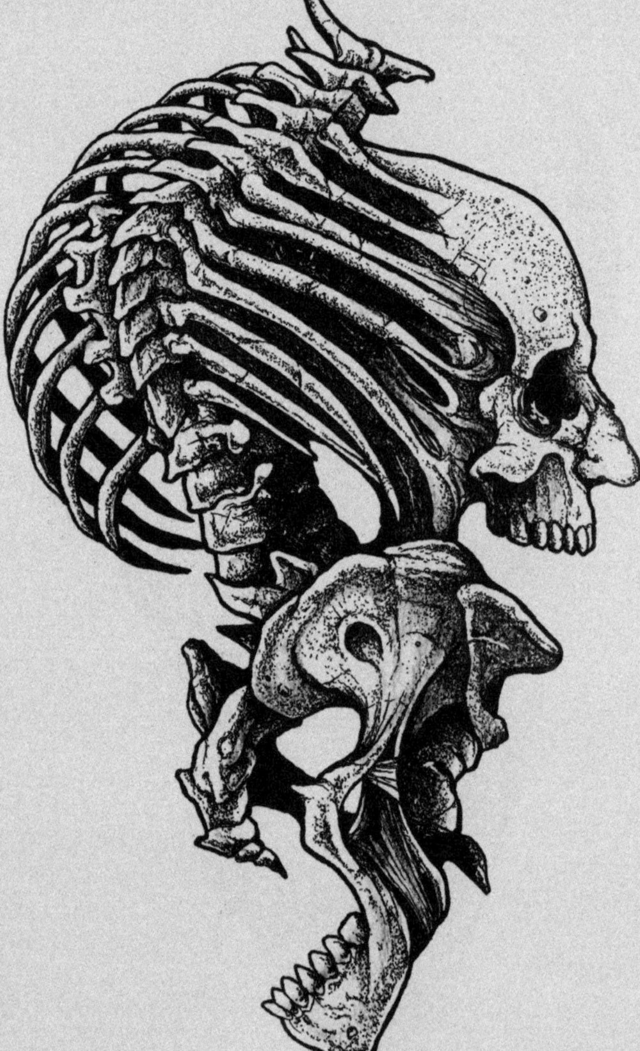

Sinpiggyhead

(81)

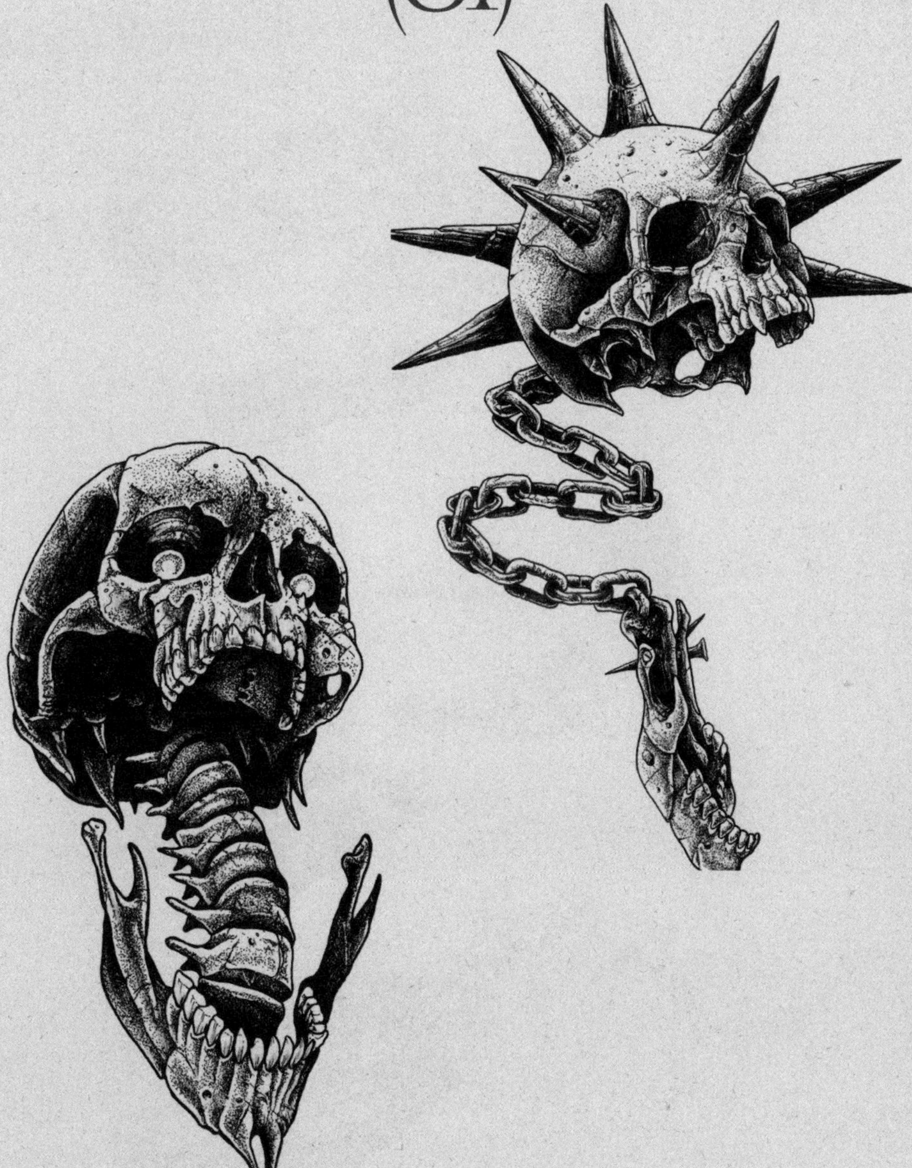

Sinpiggyhead

(82)

Sinpiggyhead

(83)

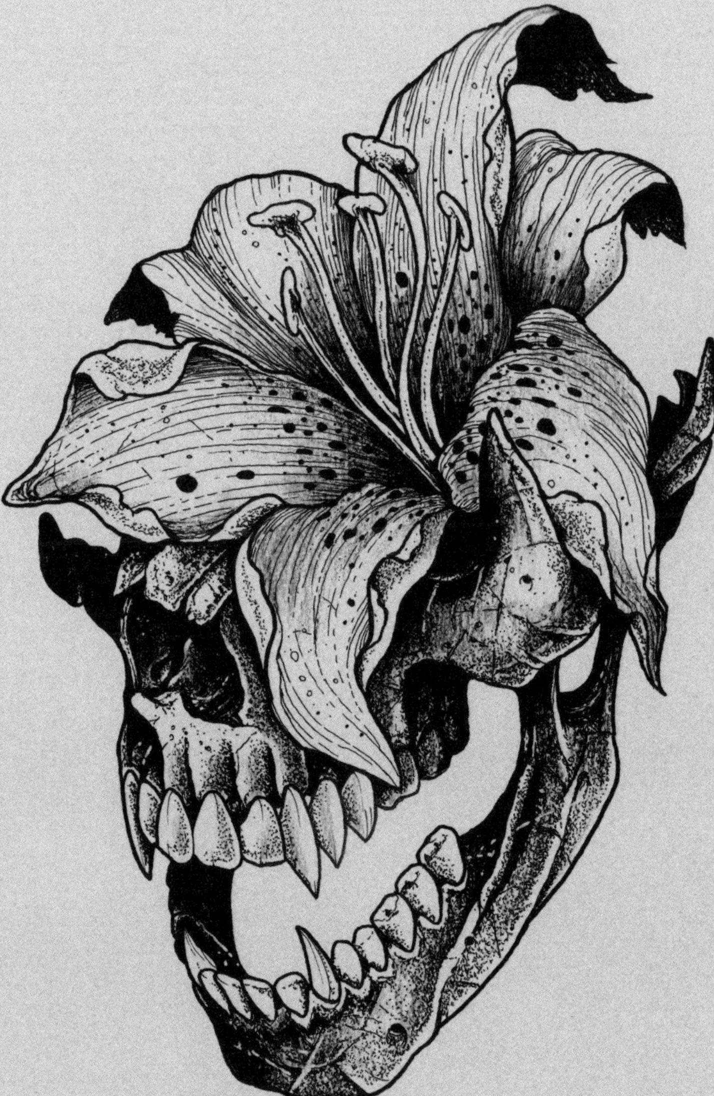

Sinpiggyhead

(84)

Apip

(85)

Apip

(86)

Apip

(87)

Apip

(88)

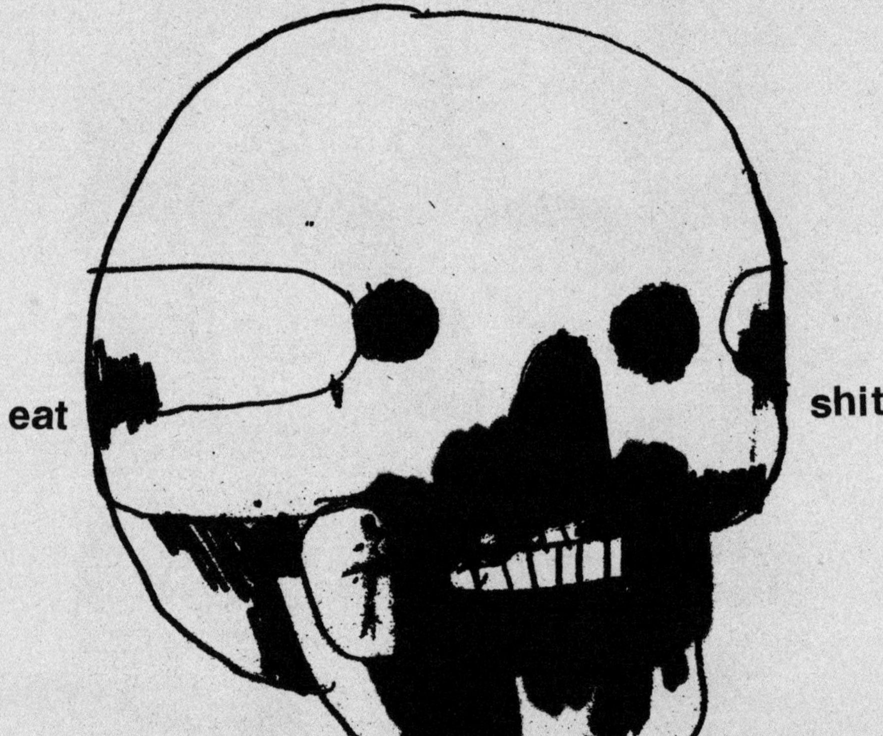

Harry Wyld

(89)

Chris Piascik

(90)

Karpichev Artem aka bth3run

(91)

Karpichev Artem aka bth3run

(92)

Gillian Wilson

(93)

Gillian Wilson

(94)

Jimi Biscuits

(95)

Jimi Biscuits

Jimi Biscuits

(97)

Jimi Biscuits

(98)

Stevie Hogan

(99)

Stevie Hogan

(100)

HELLSANDRO

HELLSANDRO

(102)

HELLSANDRO

(103)

HELLSANDRO

HELLSANDRO

ANOTHER
EMPITY
29
HELLSANDRO
SHITTY DAY

HELLSANDRO
DRUNK FOREVER

(106)

Chris Piascik

Chris Piascik

(108)

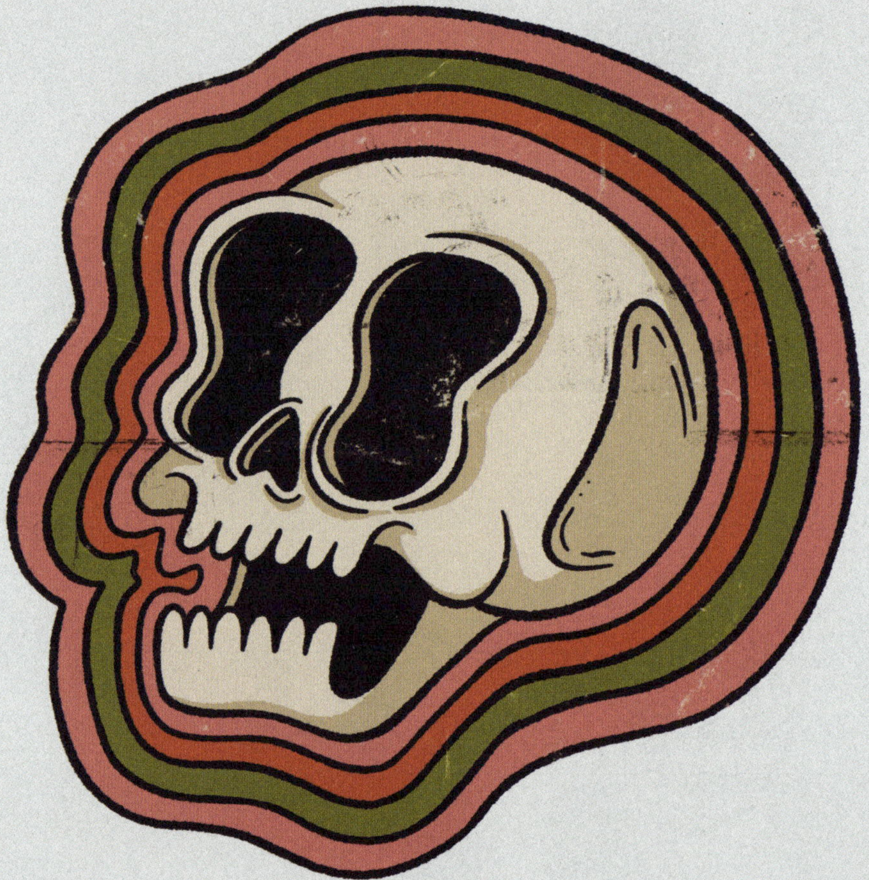

Chris Piascik

Cranial

Inspired by the cranial bones that protect the brain and form the skull's structure, this section showcases projects that delve into the core of human consciousness and the magnetic mysticism beyond - reimagining the skull as a canvas for sculptural beauty, symbolic narratives, and epic worlds born out of wild imagination.

pp.109-359

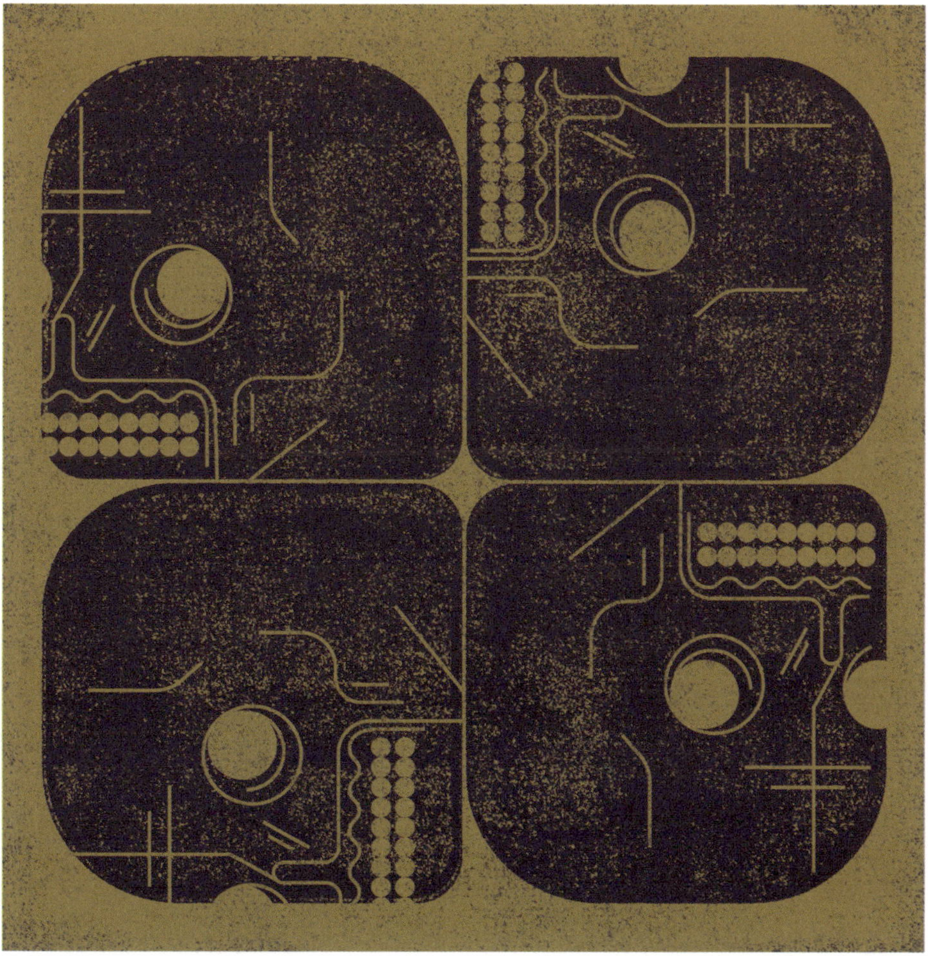

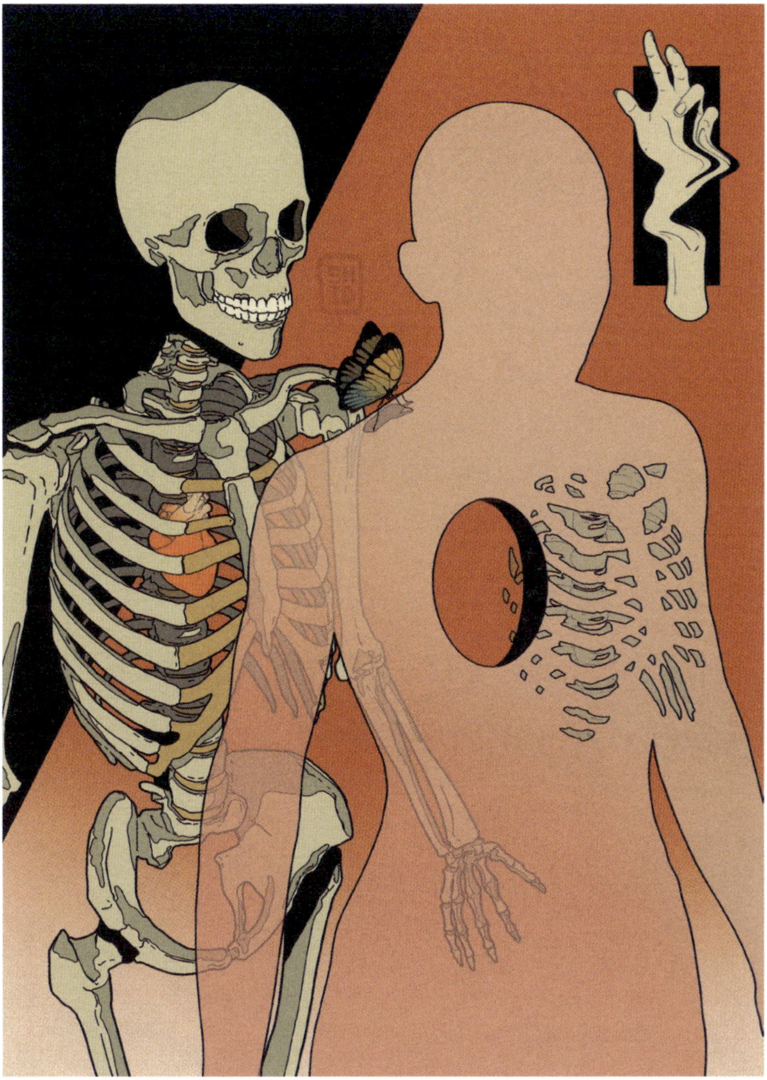

Skulls fascinate because they symbolise life's transience yet feel deeply familiar. They've long symbolised our shared mortality, stripping away external differences to reveal the bones beneath – a reminder of our unity.

– SOPHIE DONAJ –

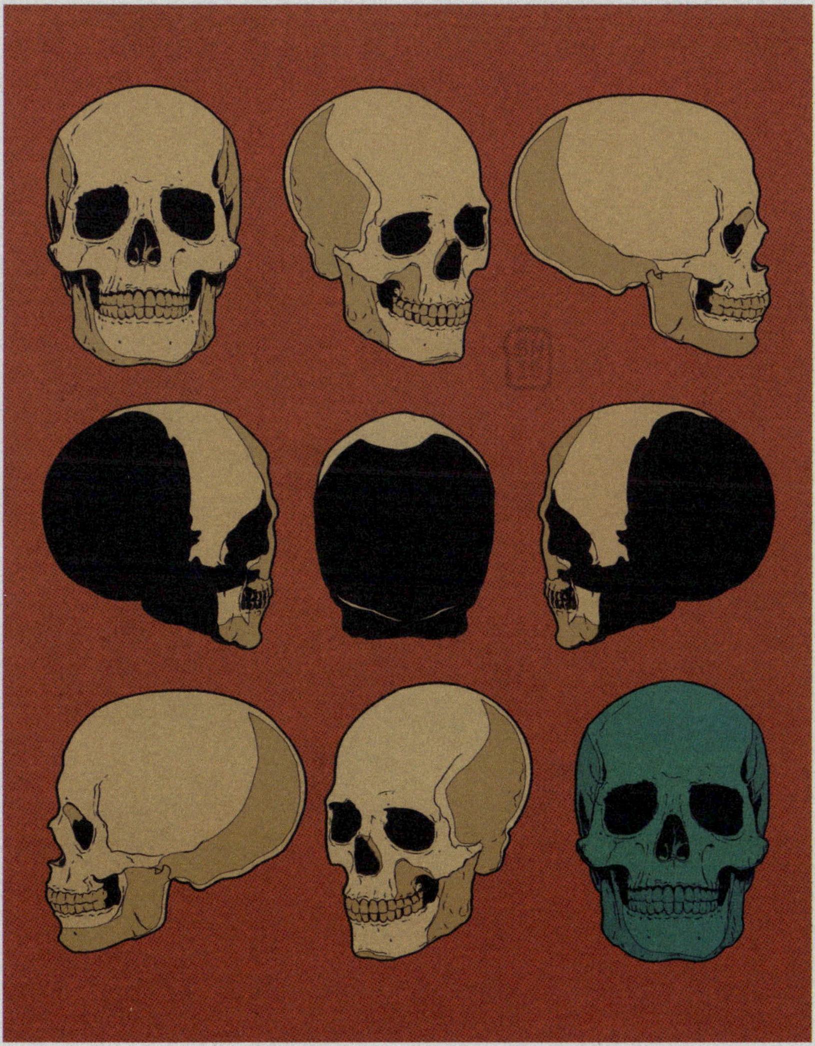

Sophie Donaj

Sophie Donaj

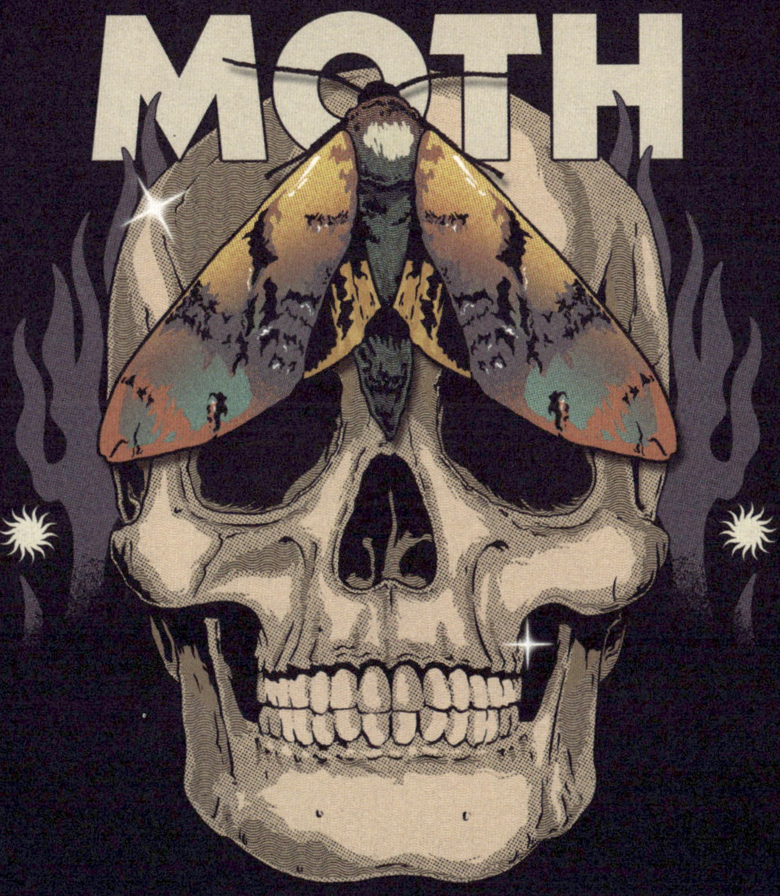

IN PENCILS WE TRUST
PROVIDENT
DISCIPLINE
19
76
HAND MADE
IS THE FUTURE
BE THE MAGIC NOT THE ILLUSION

ARS LONGA · VITA BREVIS

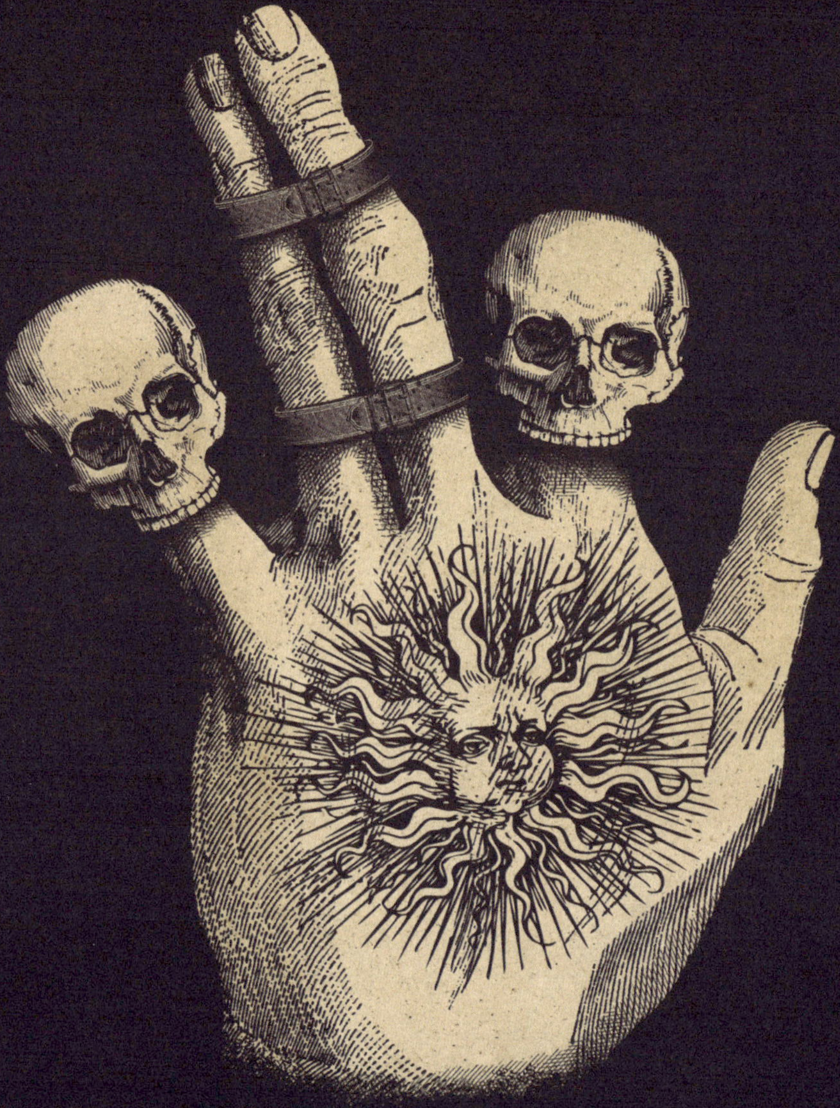

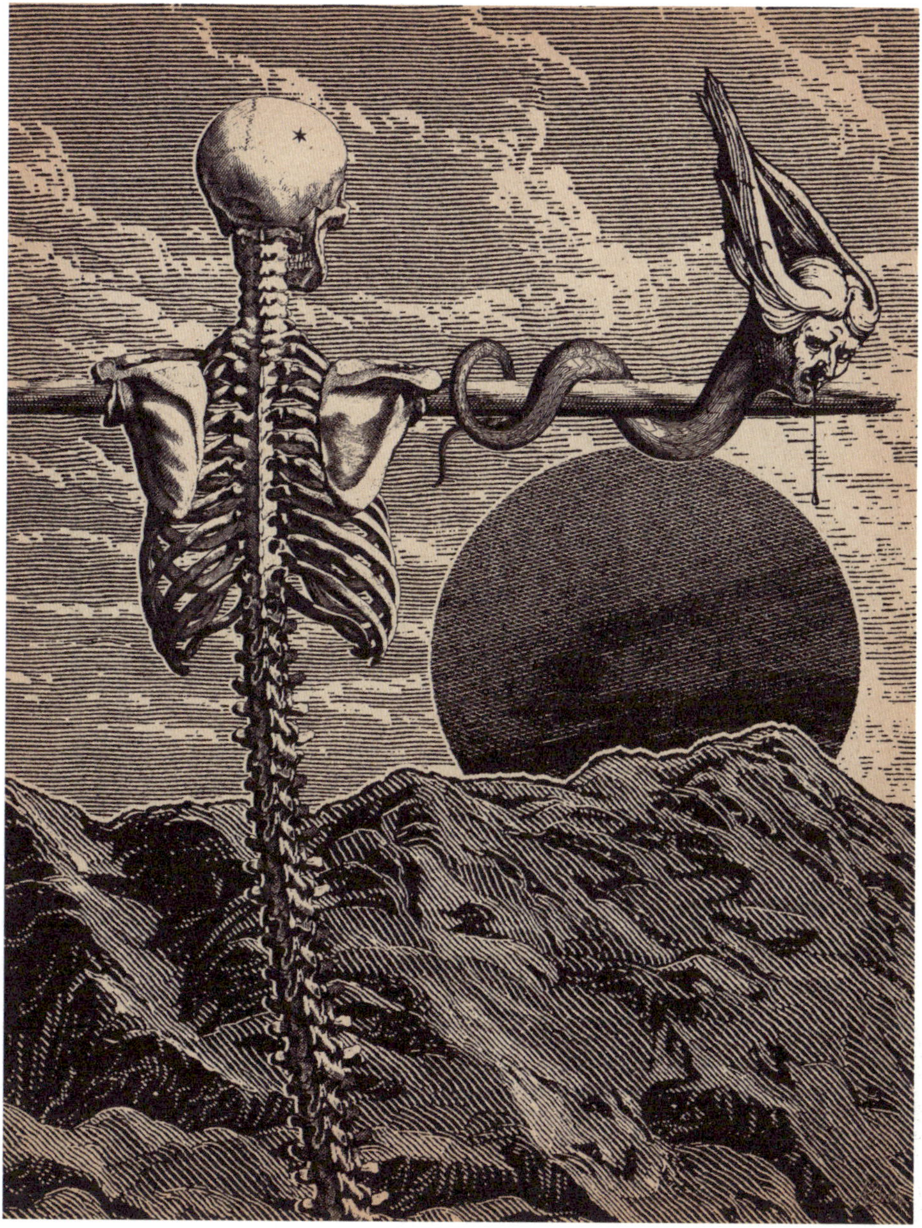

Andrew Blucha

Skulls are symbolically rich and a haunting reminder of life's fleeting nature. Though simple in form, they serve as a powerful means to convey complex human emotions.

– GILLIAN WILSON –

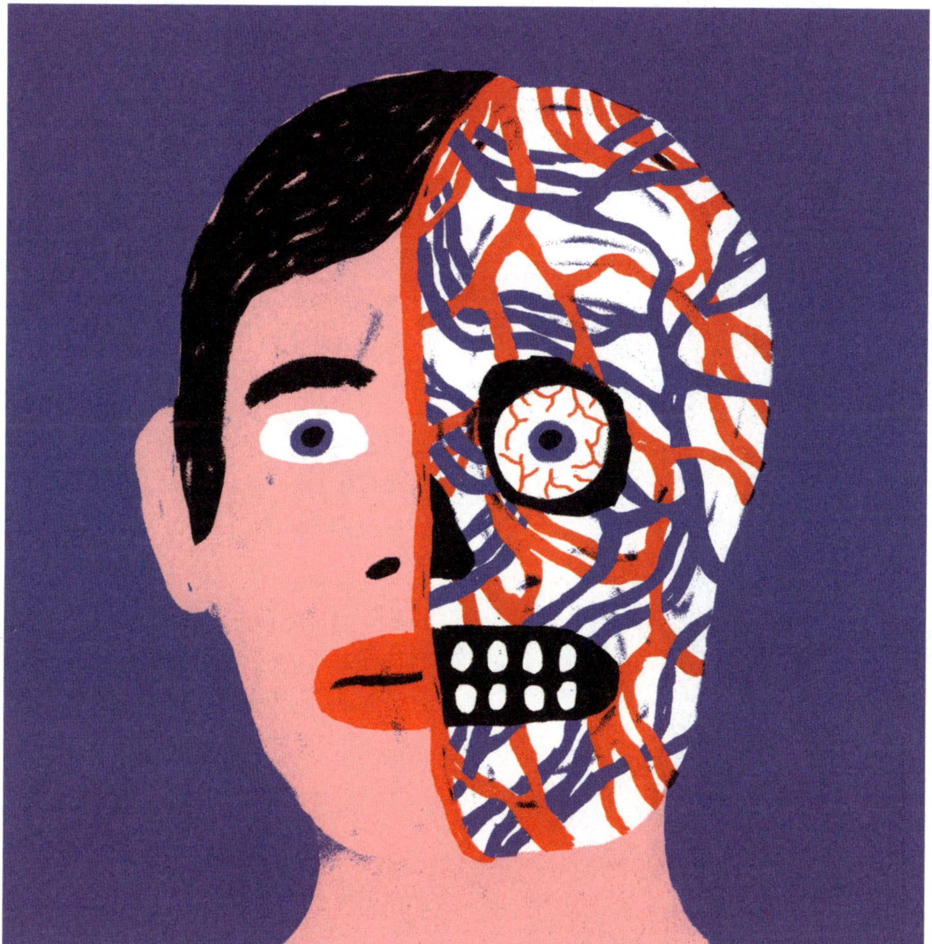

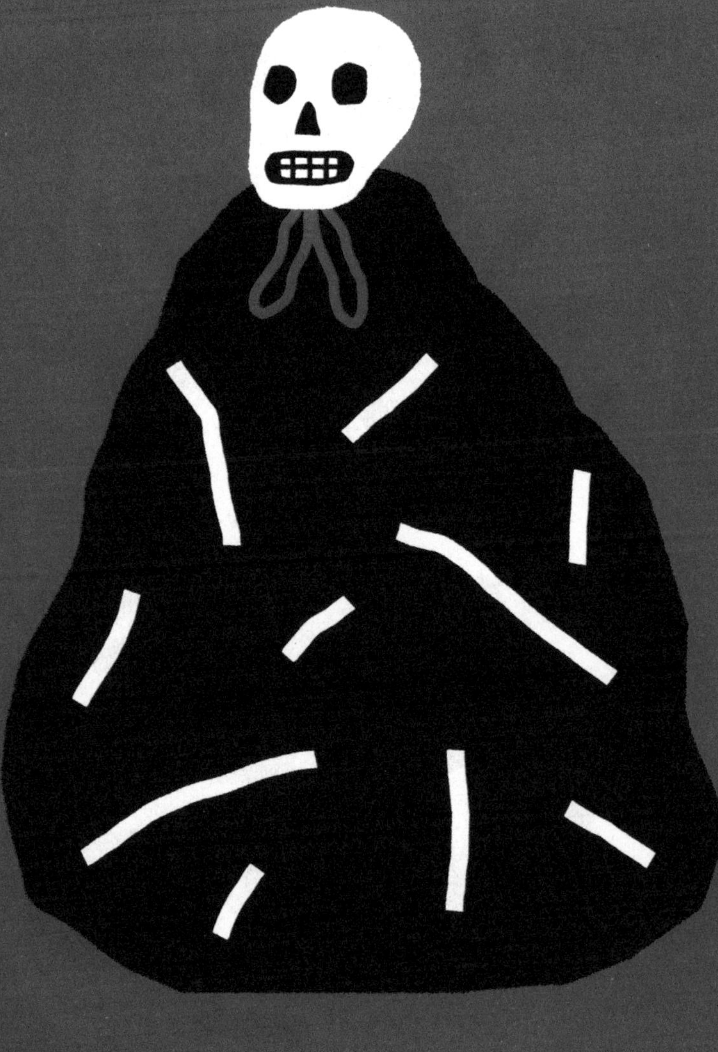

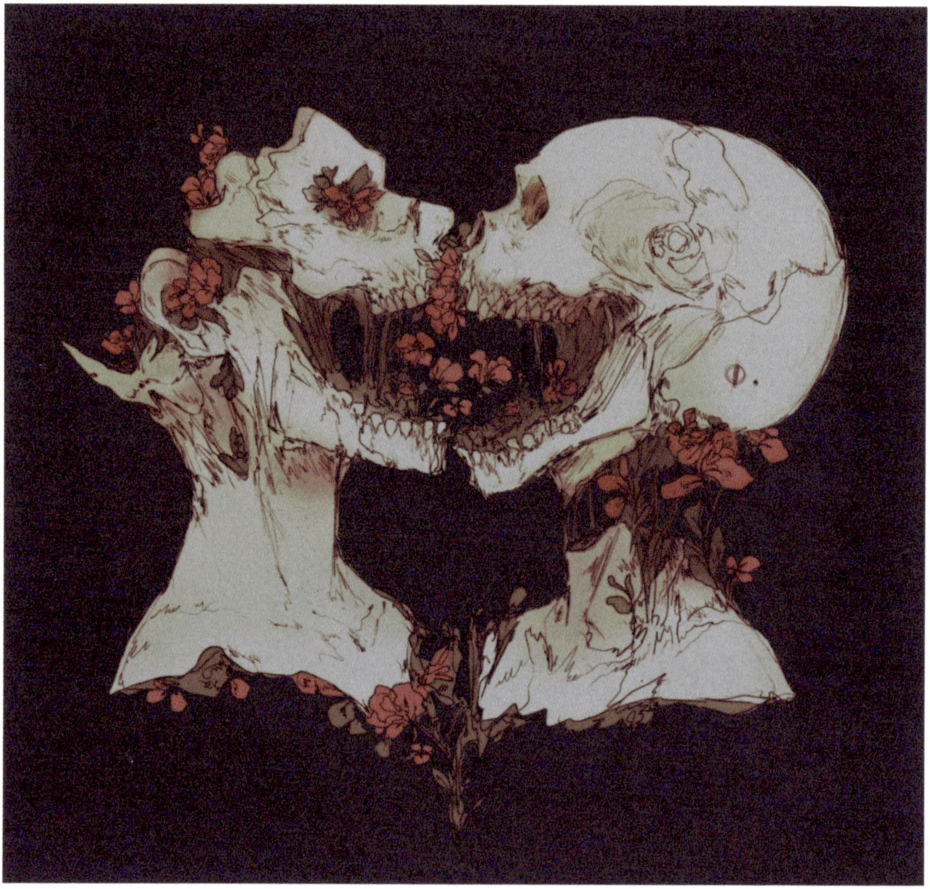

Ungfio

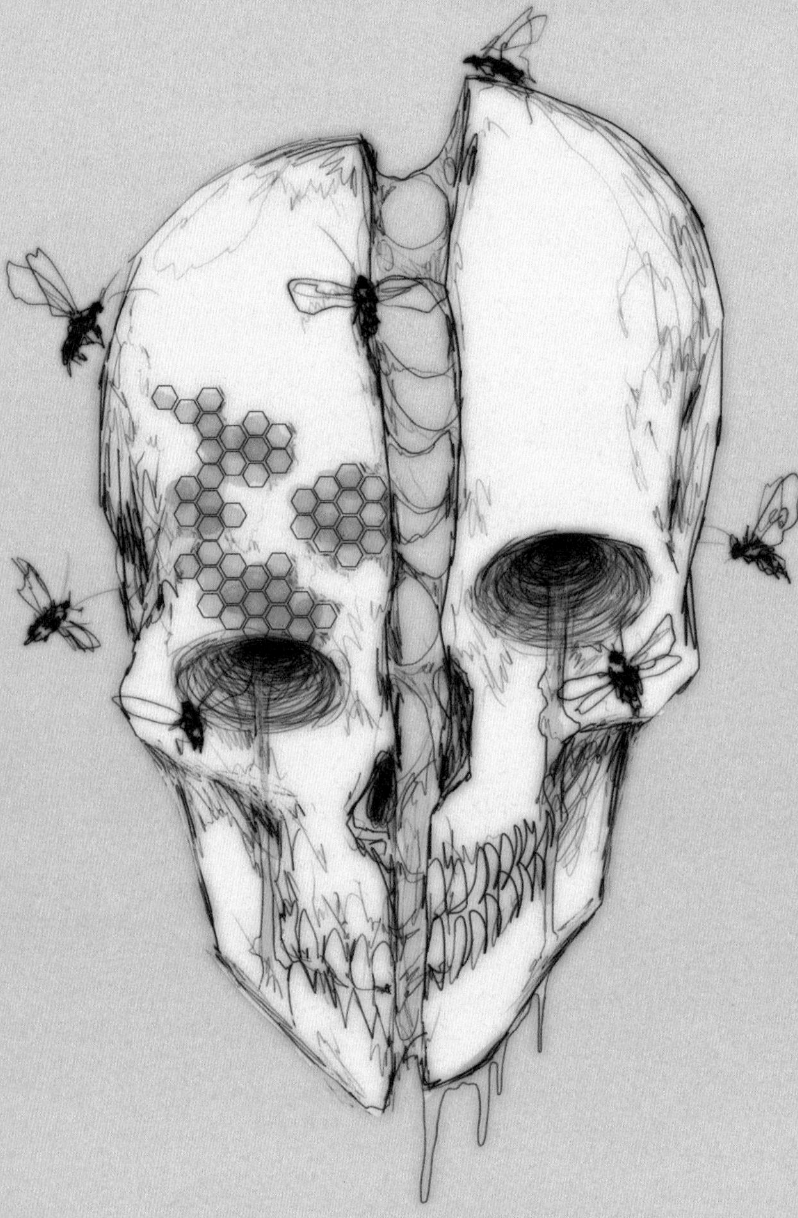

BMO

Ungfio

The anonymity and dramatic intensity of skulls offer viewers great freedom of interpretation. Some see them as morbid, while others perceive them through a more childlike or naïve lens. Their curves, complexity, and texture—and the way light brings them to life—make them an ideal subject for painting and art in general.

— ADRIEN CONRAD —

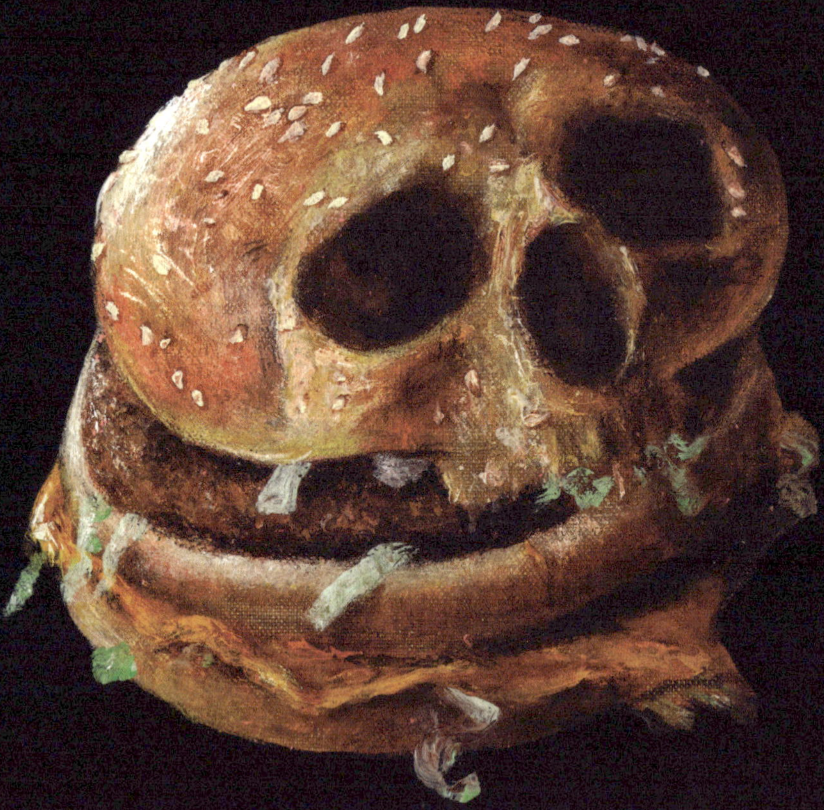

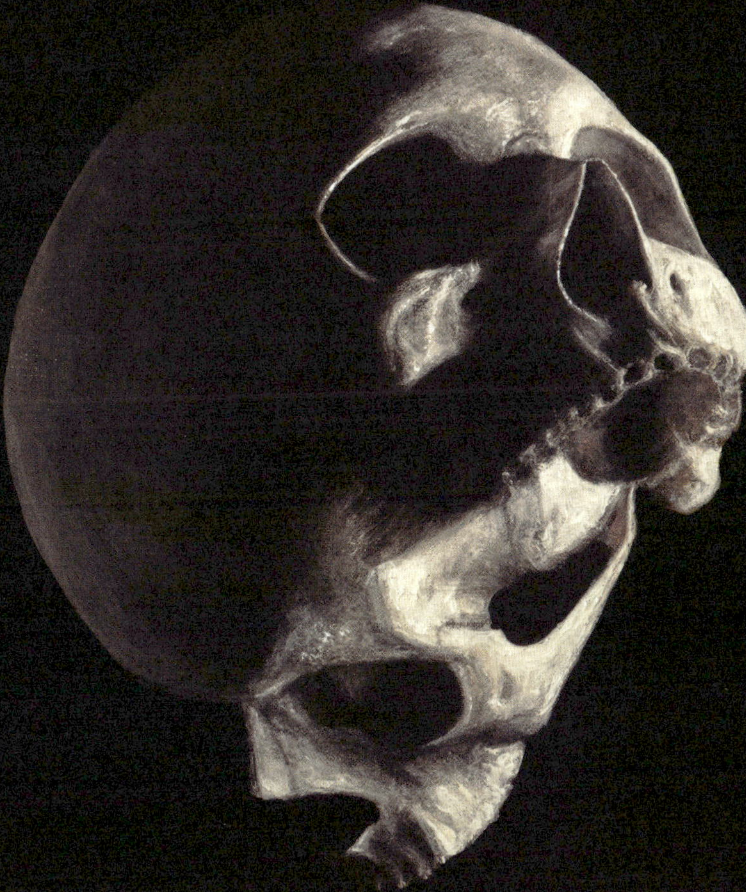

Michael Reeder

1982

The Third Transit

MORS
MIHI
LVCVM

Skulls are a forensic record of your unique identity – like a cave artist pressing their hand to a wall and blowing yellow ochre around it to say, "I lived." It makes life feel a little less meaningless and laughs in the face of the cosmic joke of mortality.

– ALEXANDER DE CADENET –

Vladimir Chebakov

Vladimir Chebakov

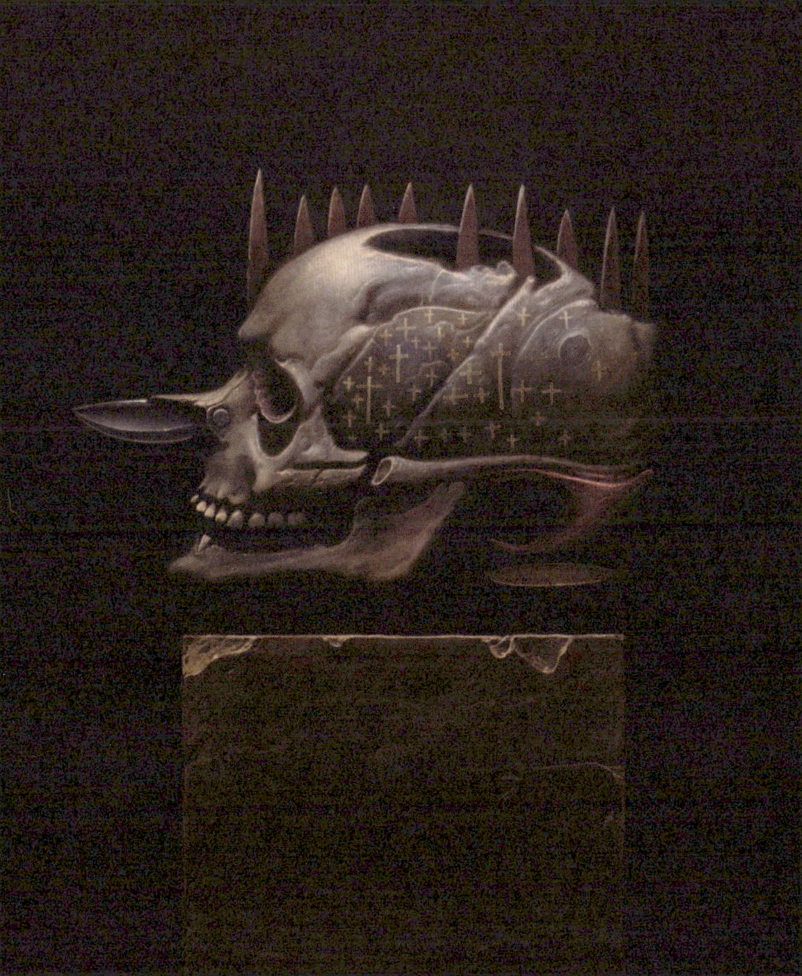

PEDRO
CORREA 20

PEDRO CORREA 20

PEDRO CORREIA 20

PEDRO CORREA
2017

CHARLIE

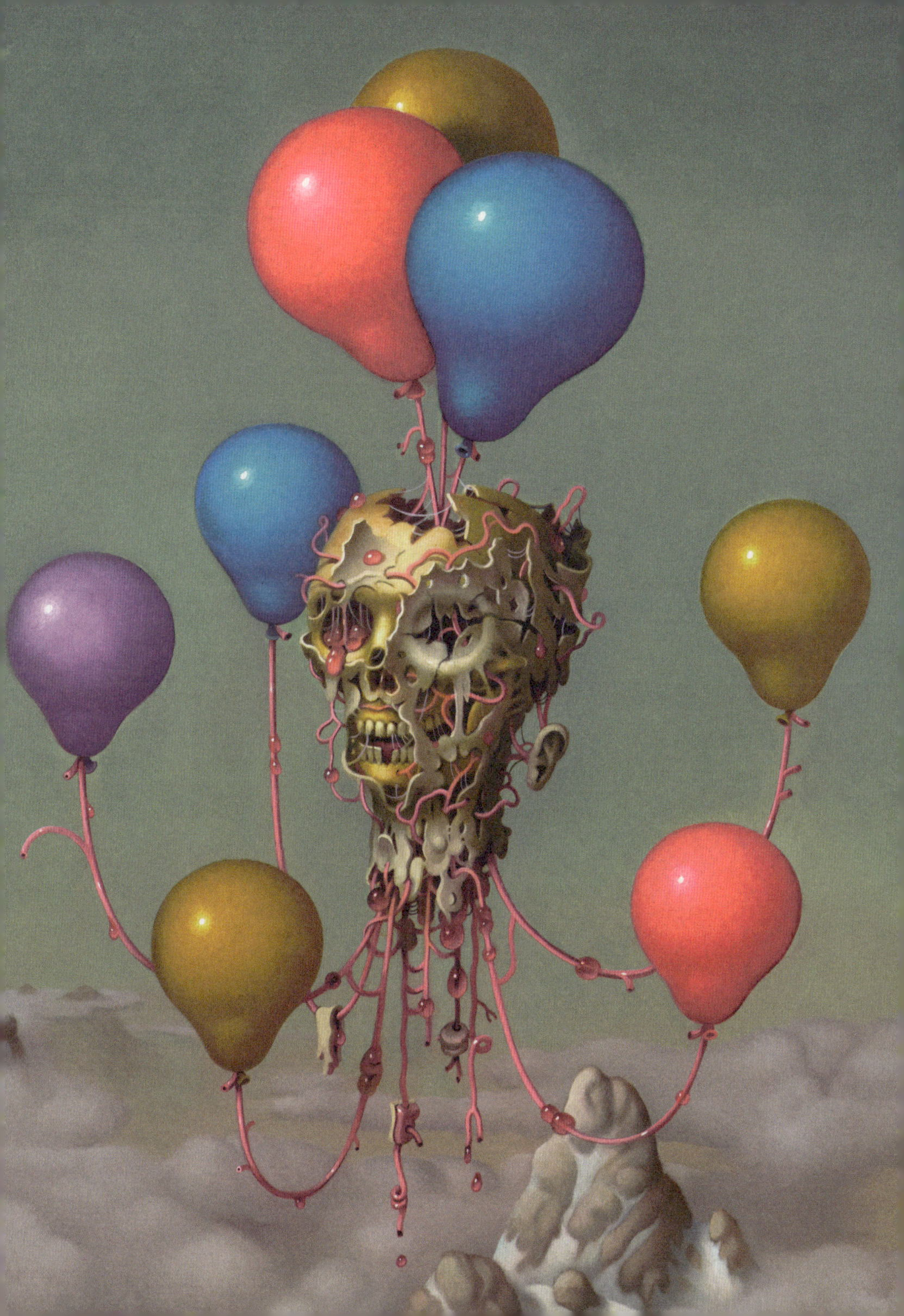

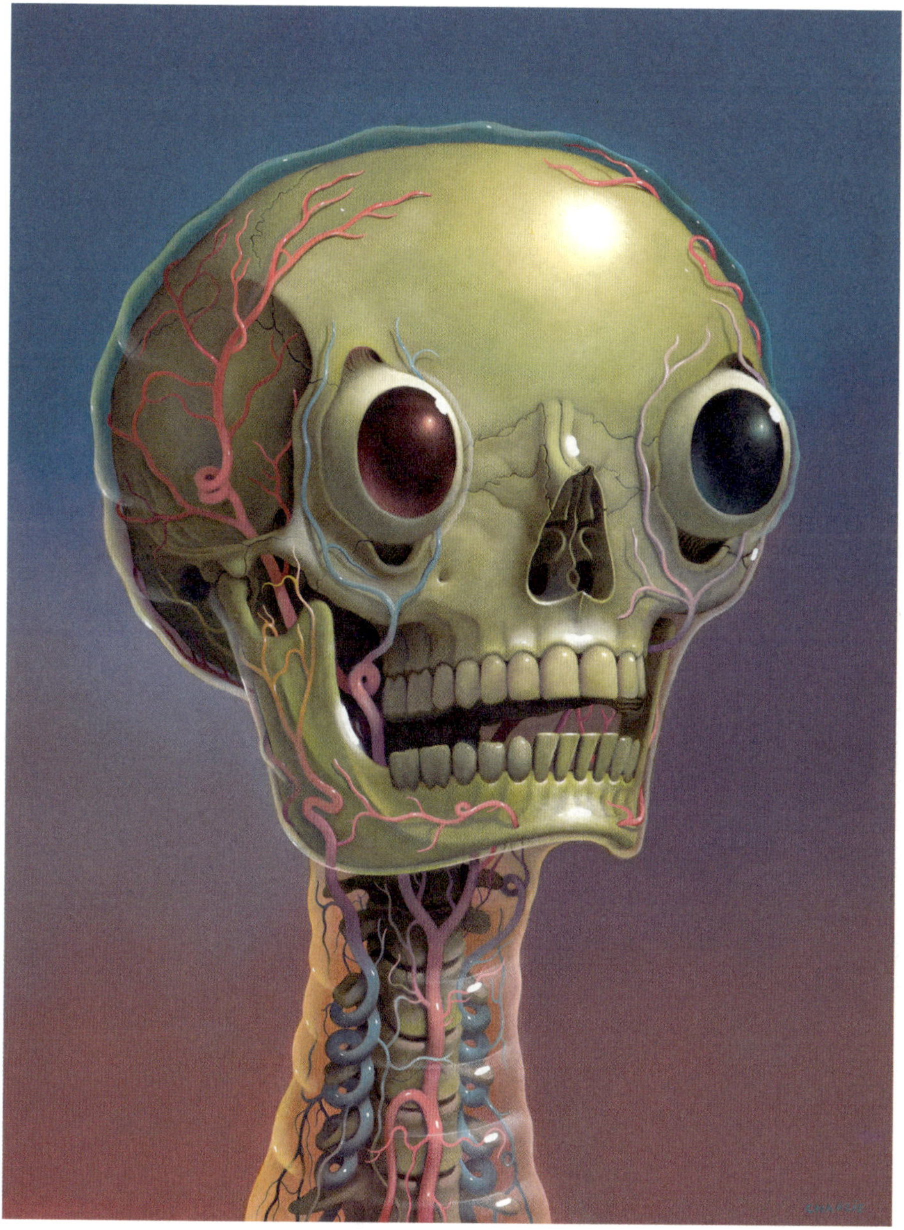

ANDIE

ANDIE

ANDIE

ANDIE

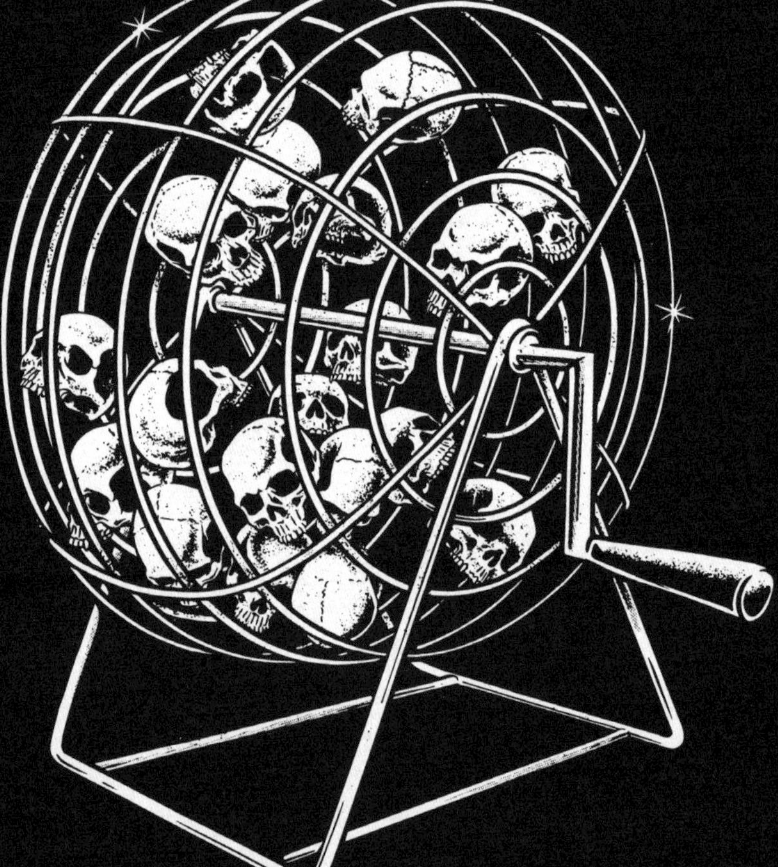

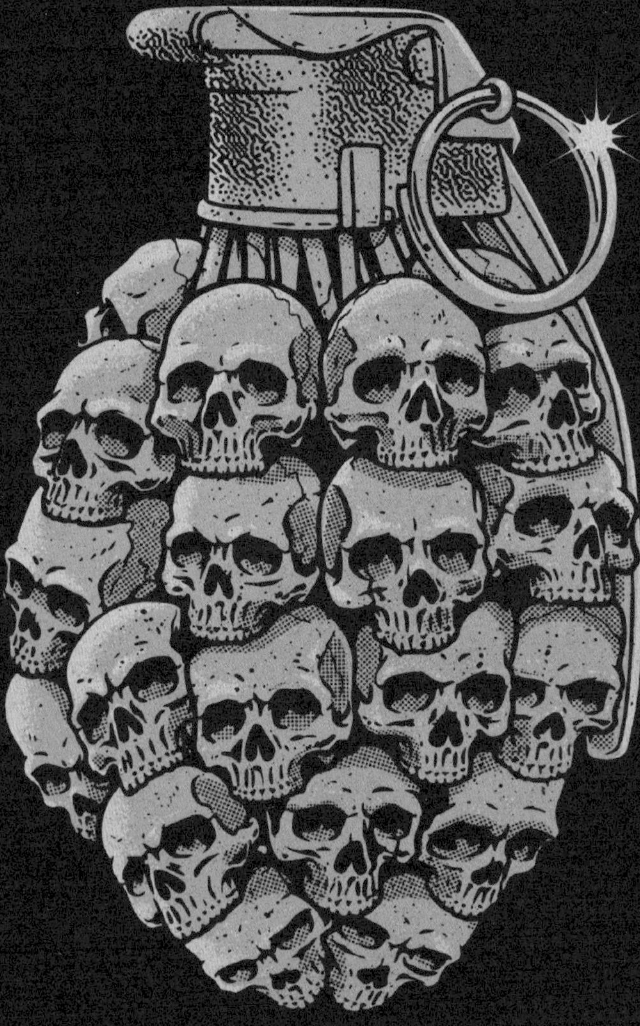

Heeey! Design

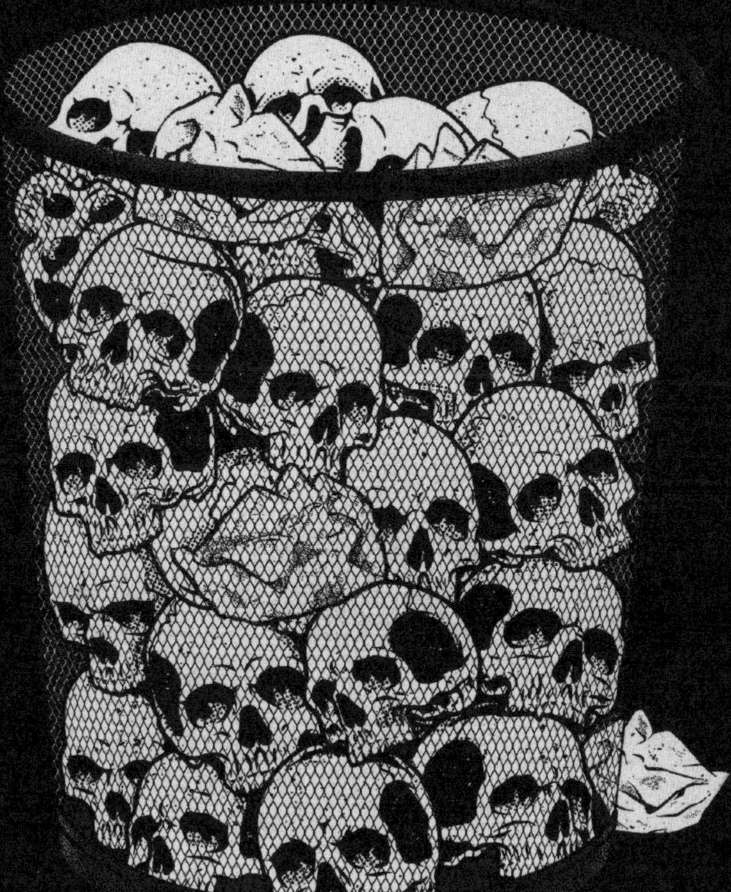

The skull is our silent echo on Earth – a fragile reminder of impermanence, yet also a timeless muse: an aesthetic vessel that has inspired artists since the dawn of art.

– ARTUR SOLETSKYI –

Emerald Barkley

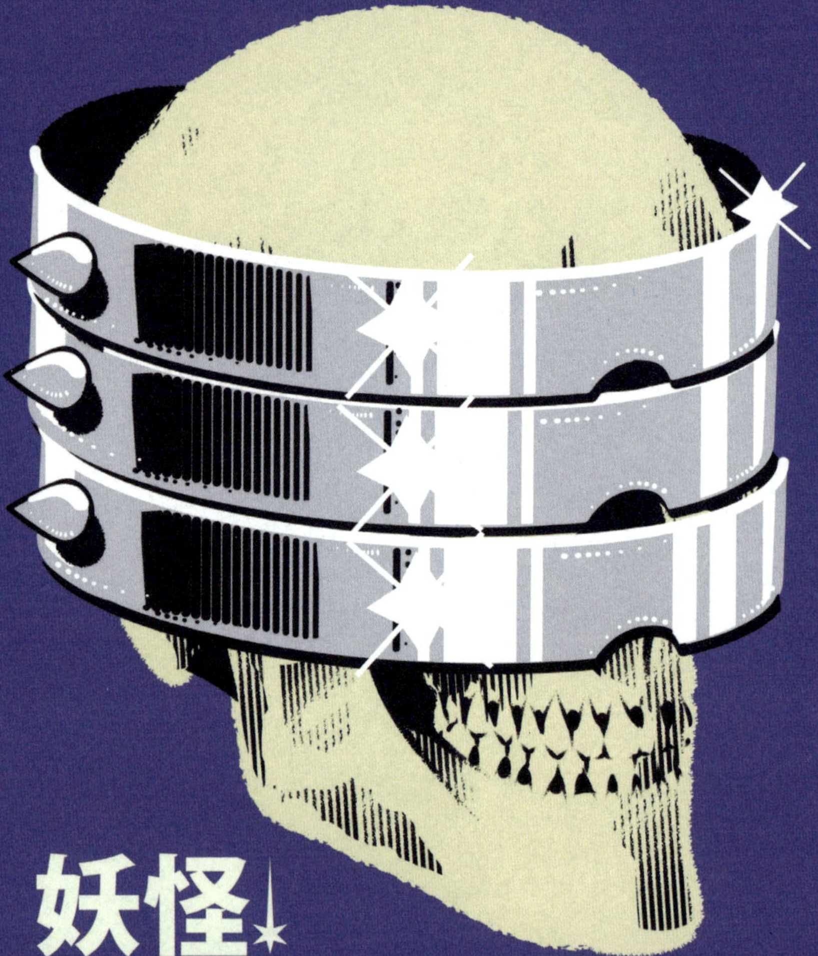
妖怪

Manuel Cetina

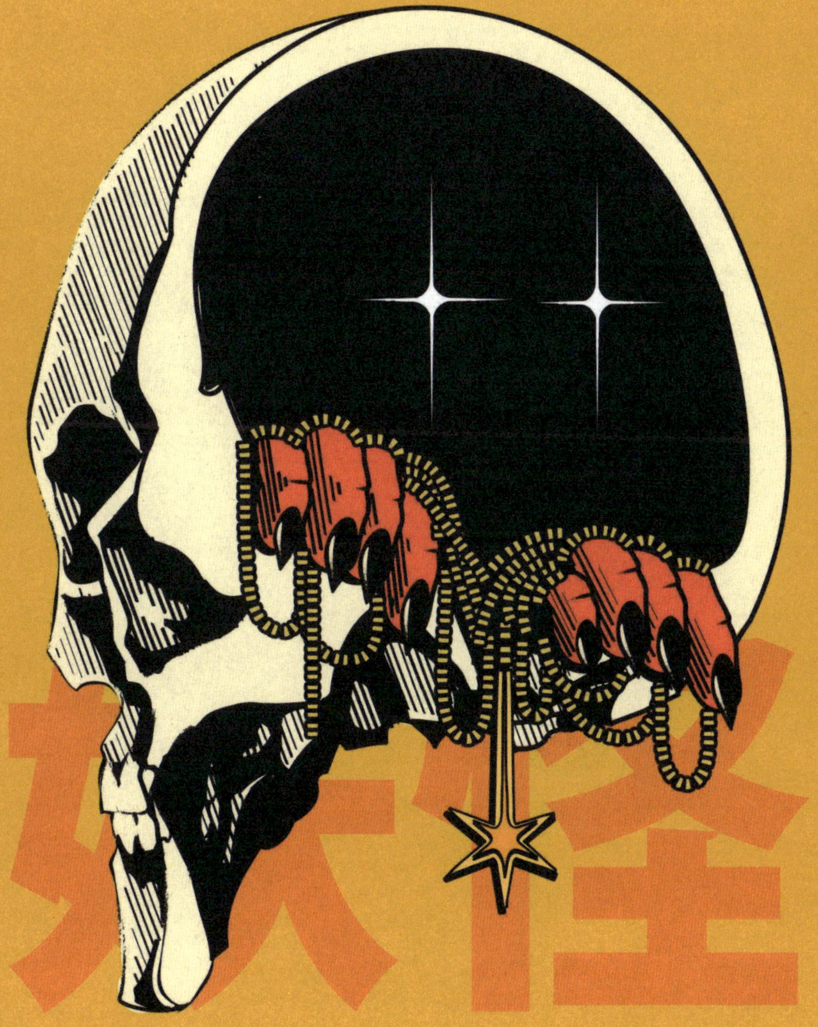

Manuel Cetina

妖怪!

241

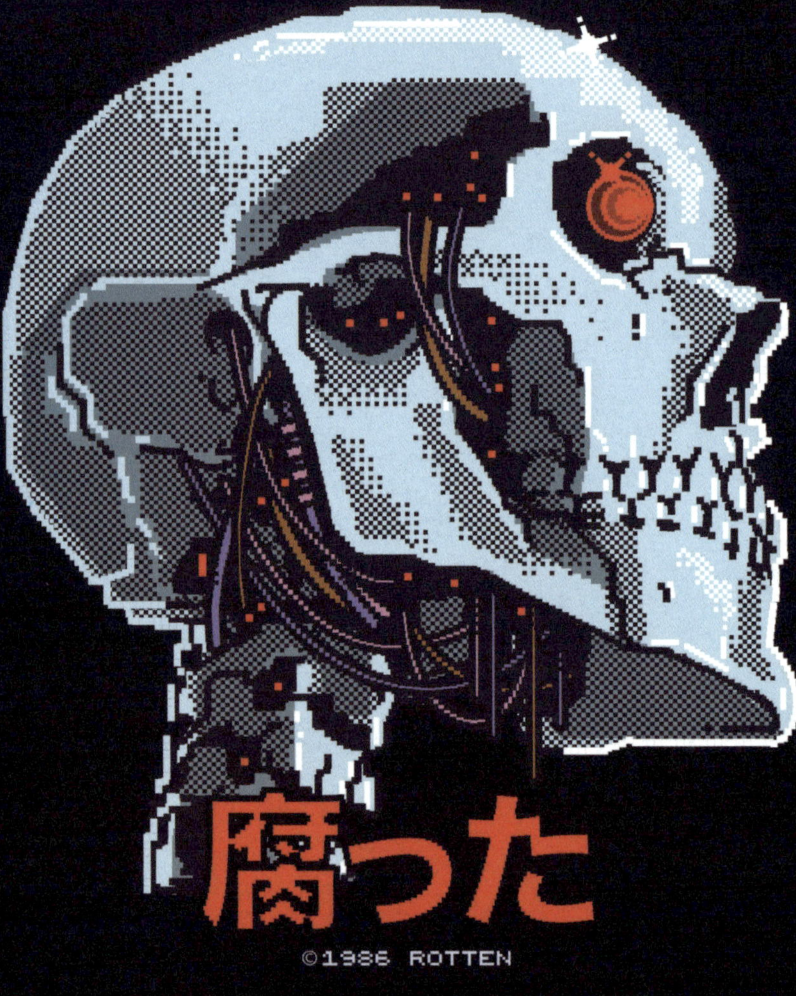
腐った
©1986 ROTTEN

Manuel Cetina

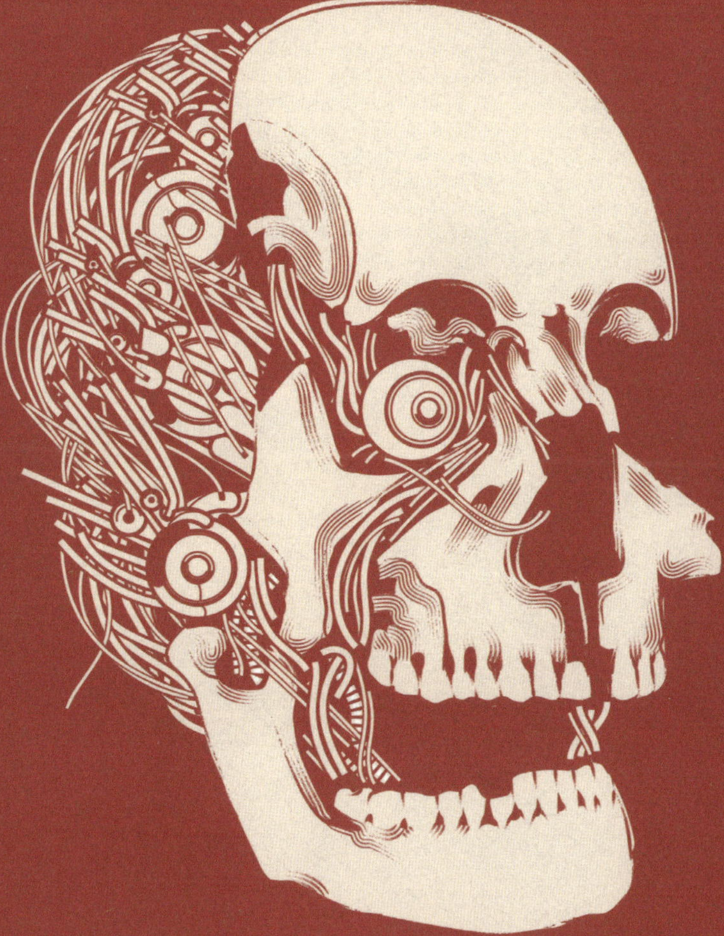

腐った

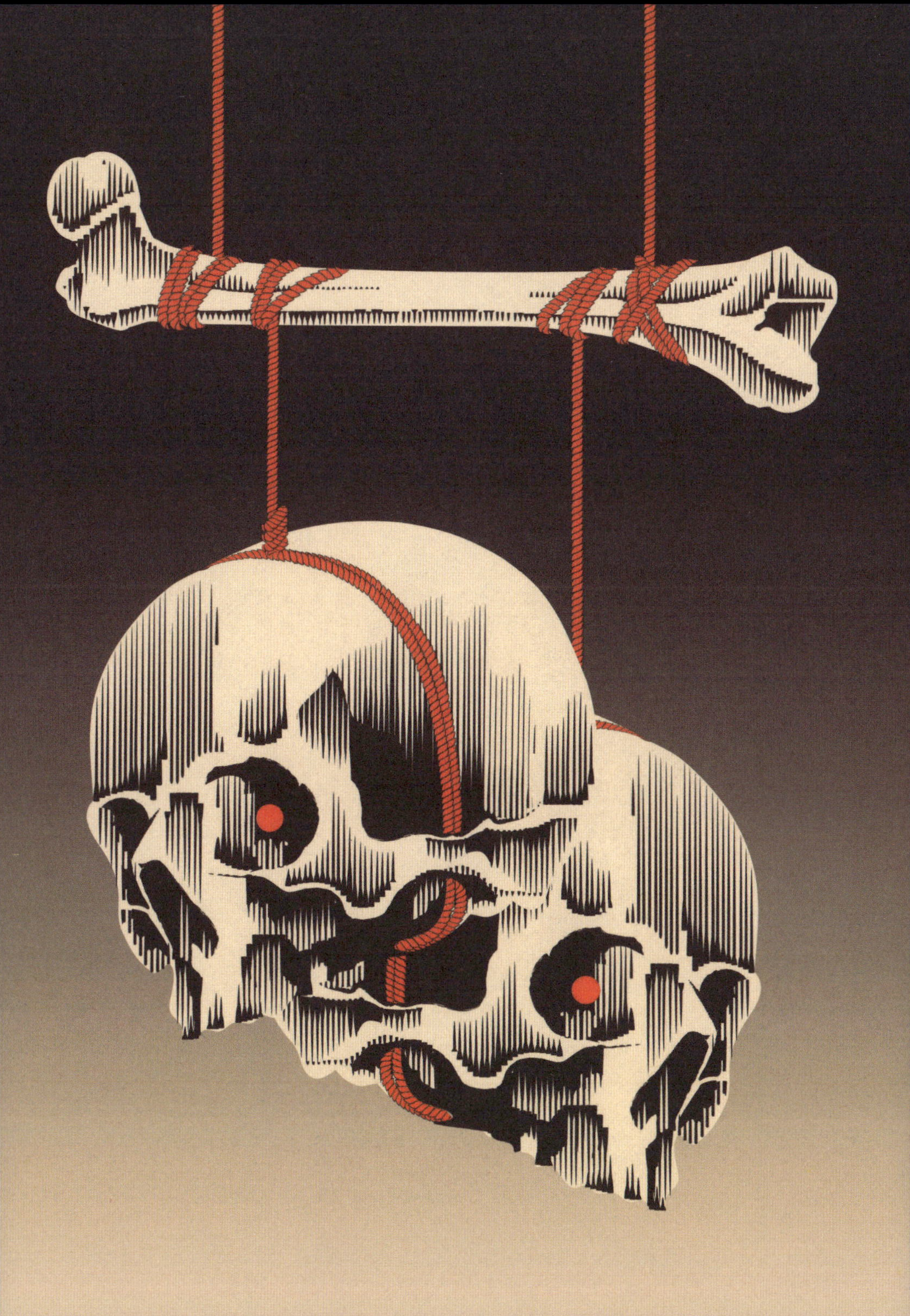

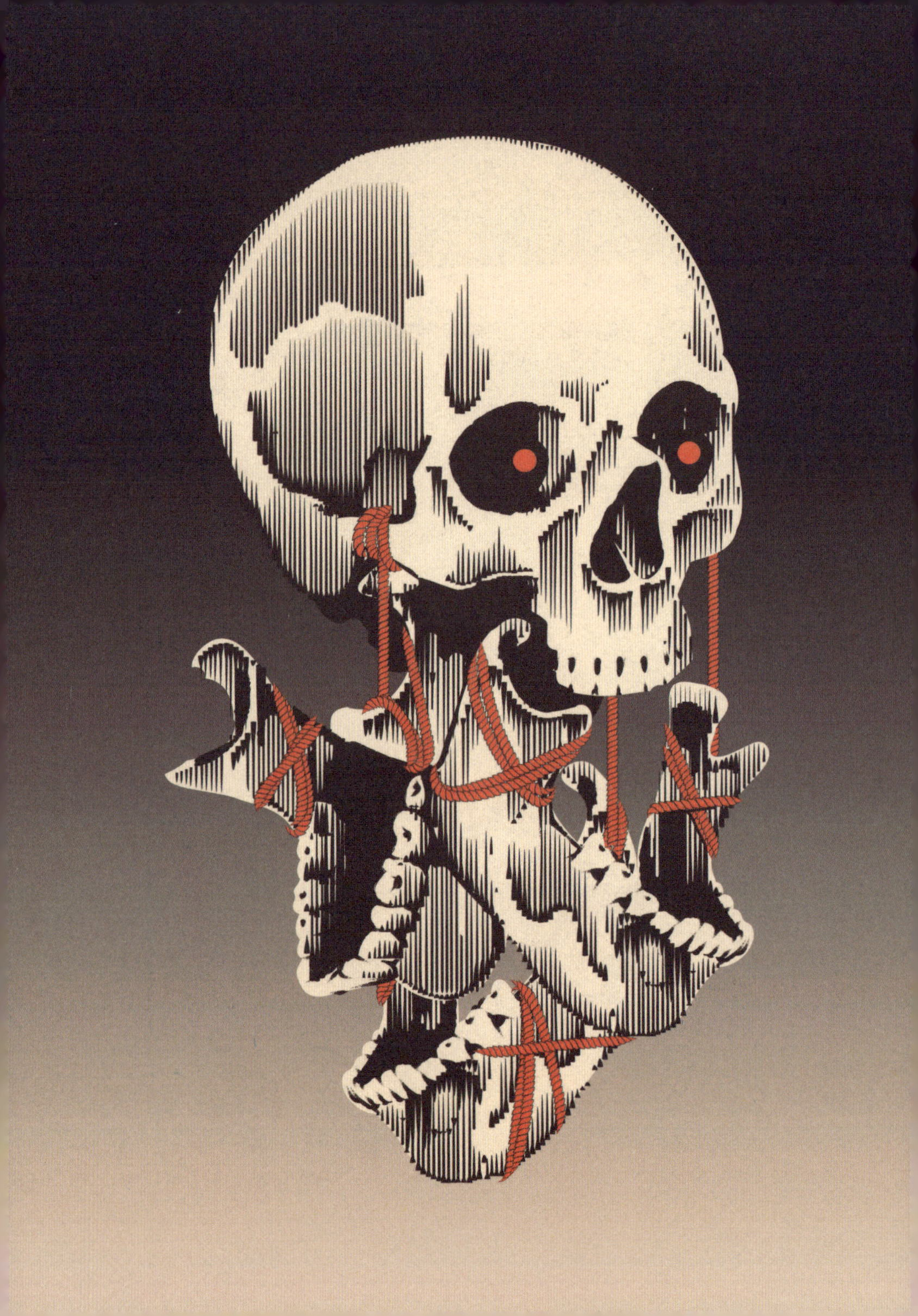

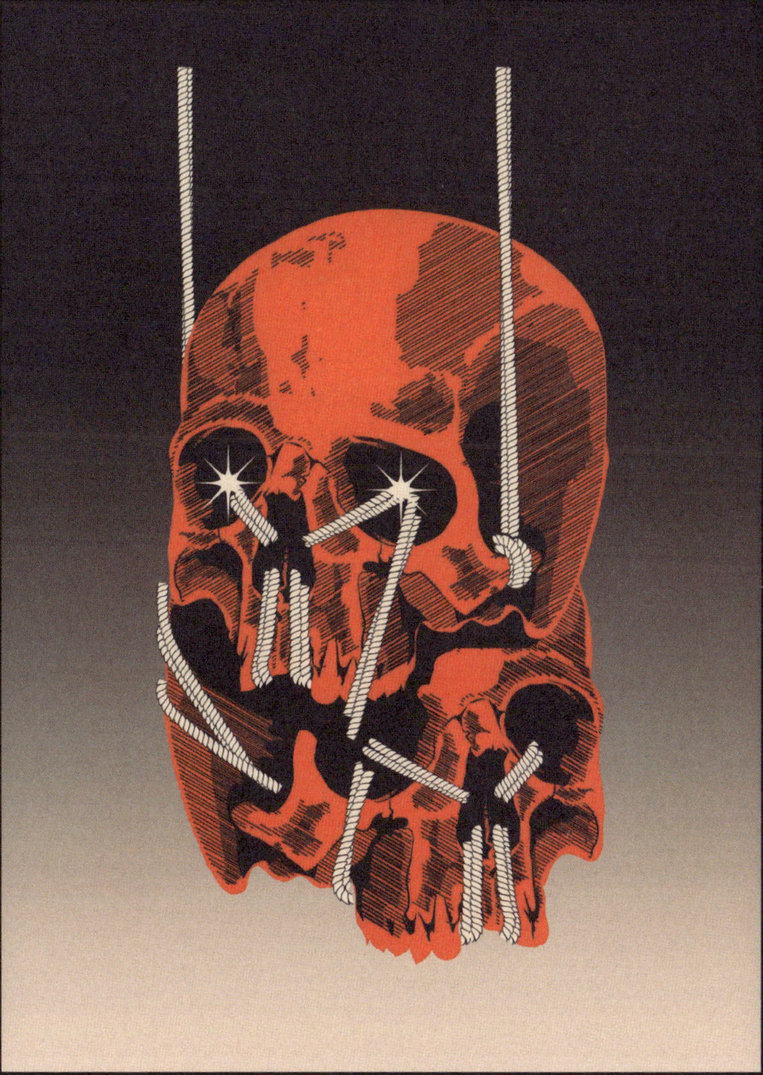

Manuel Cetina

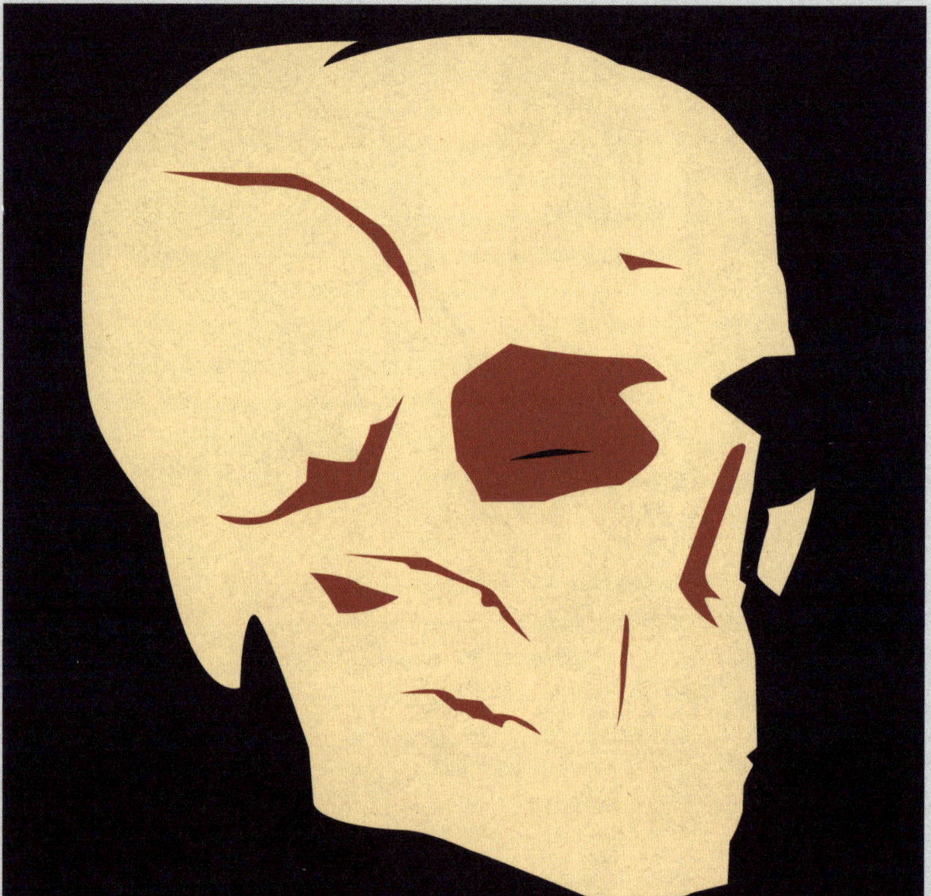

Artur Soletskyi

Stuart Morris

Skulls, shared by all humans, evoke both spiritual depth and universal intrigue. Their geometric structure invites endless stylistic interpretations, ranging from playful and curious to frightening and grotesque.

— CHARLIE IMMER —

I HATE PIKACHU

HELL YEAH!!

PUF

RESCUE

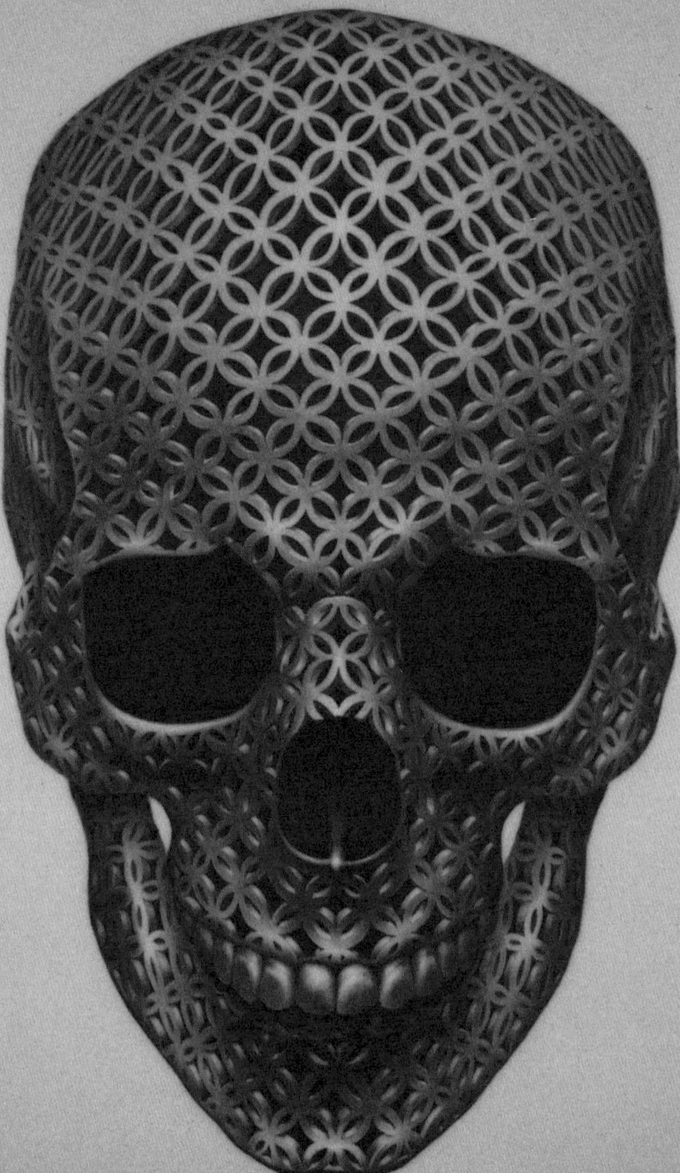

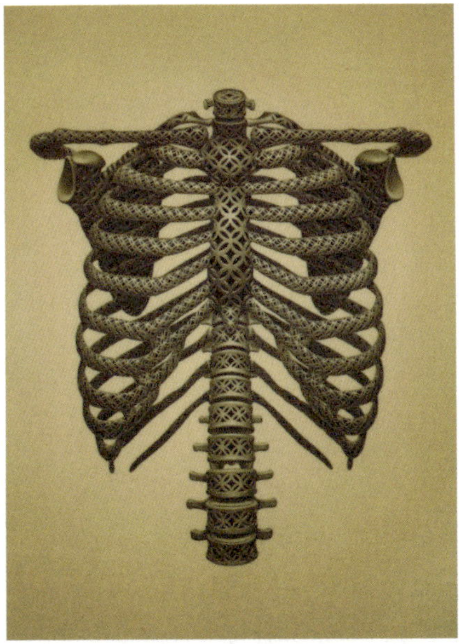

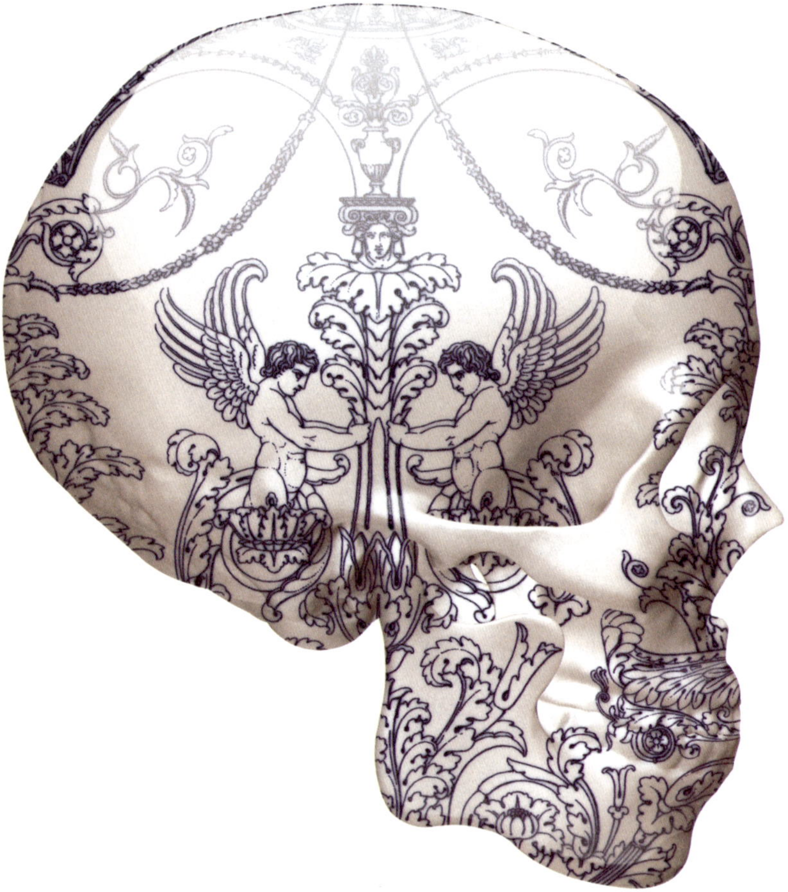

Magnus Gjoen

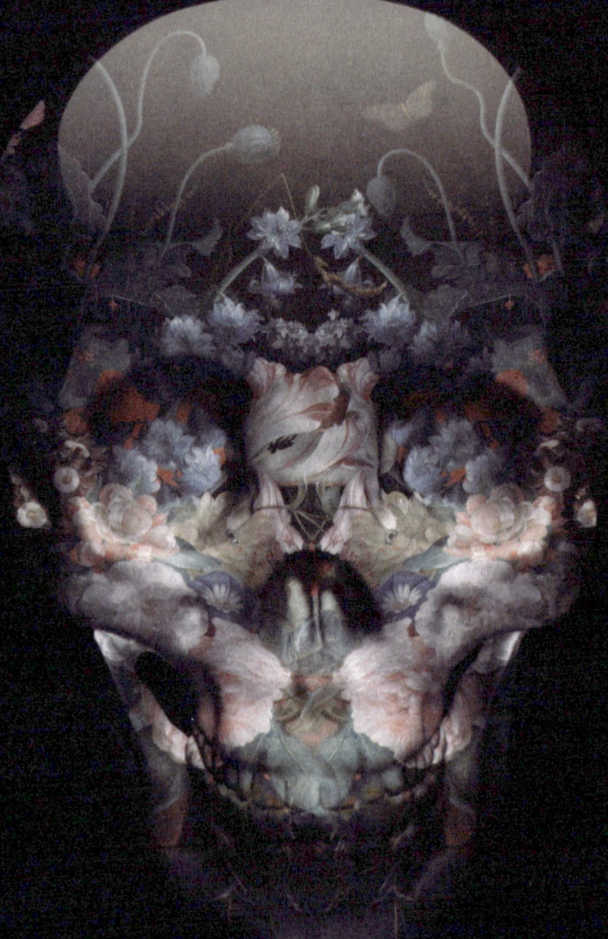

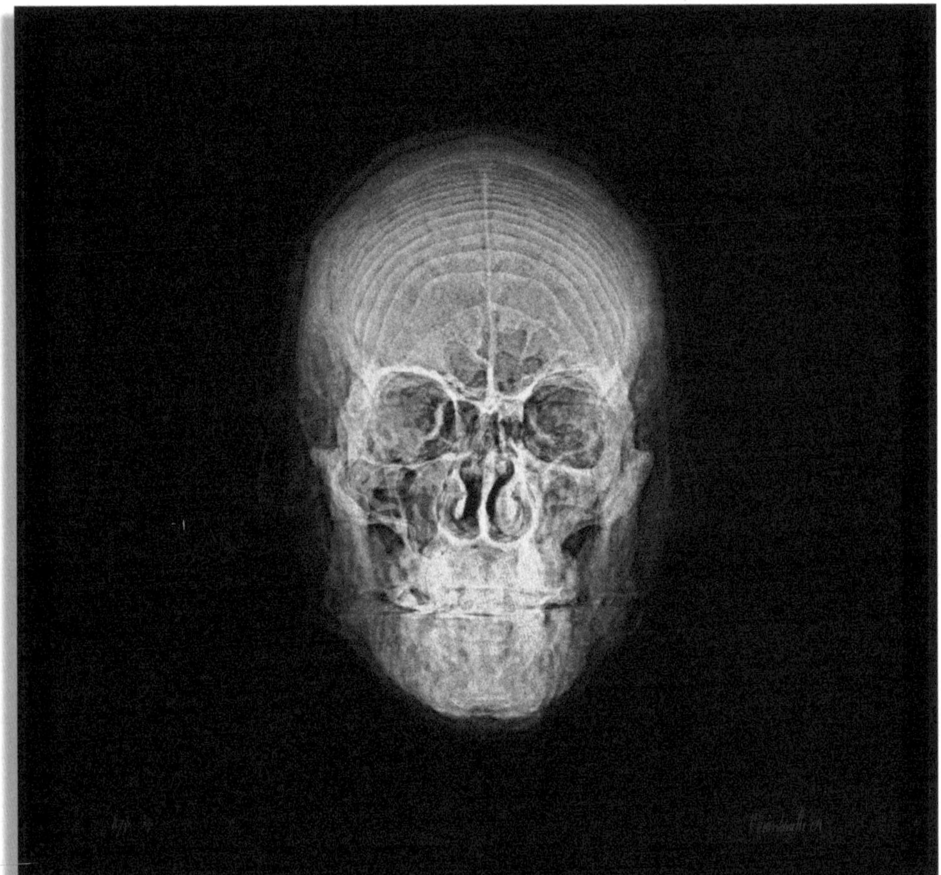

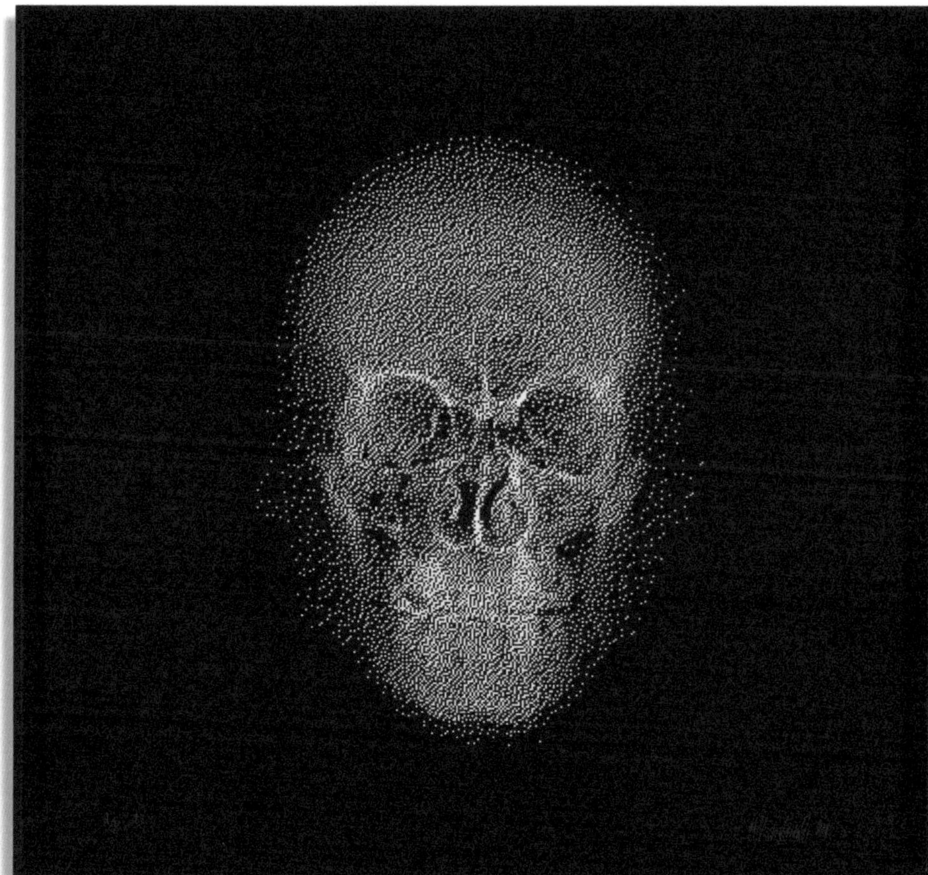

VOX

Tyler Spangler

Tyler Spangler

Tyler Spangler

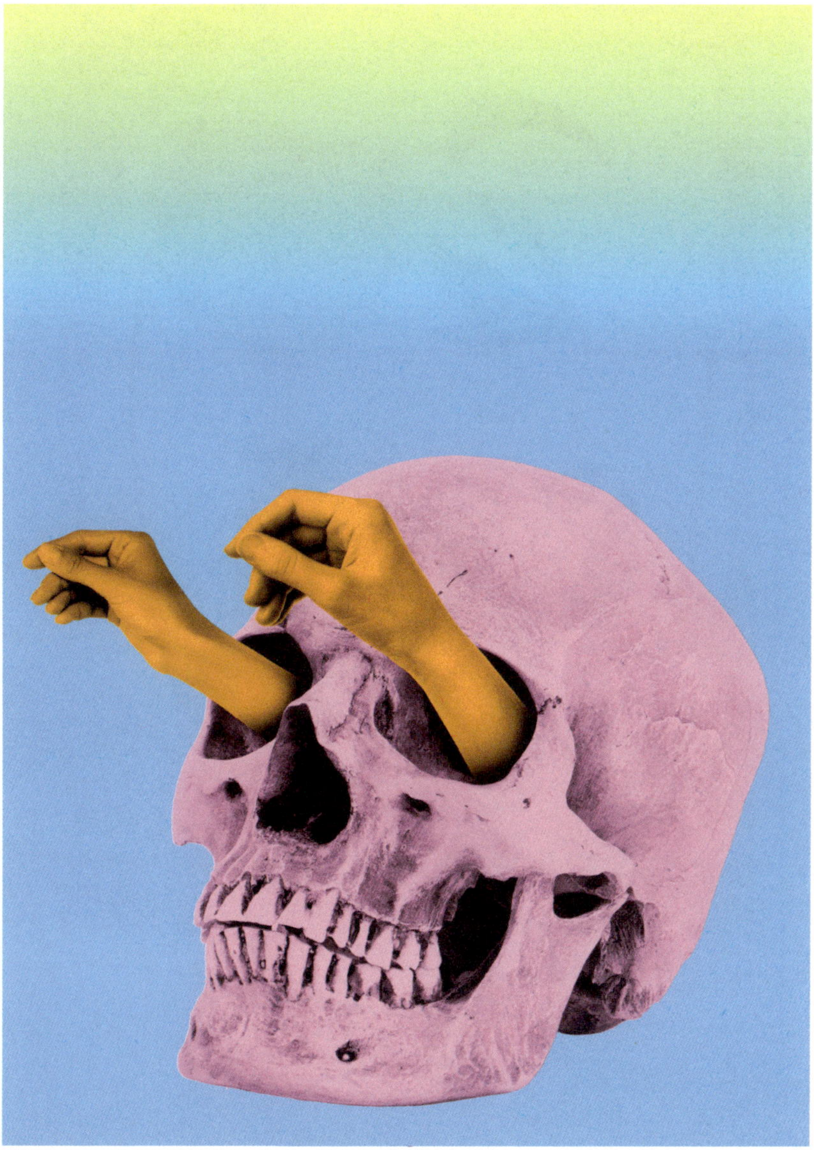

Harry Wyld

Our fascination with skulls reflects humanity's enduring need to confront both the fragility and beauty of life. Across eras and cultures, the skull acts as a mirror of our condition, reminding us that we are temporary yet part of something larger and eternal.

— HEEEY! DESIGN —

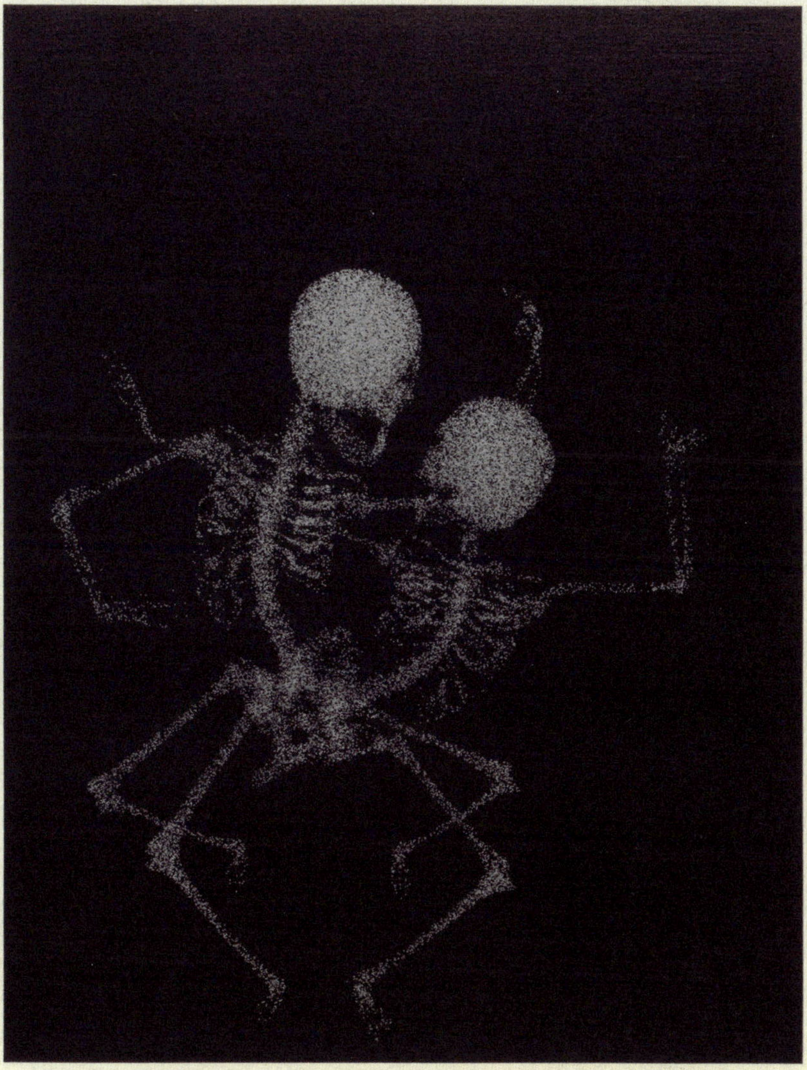

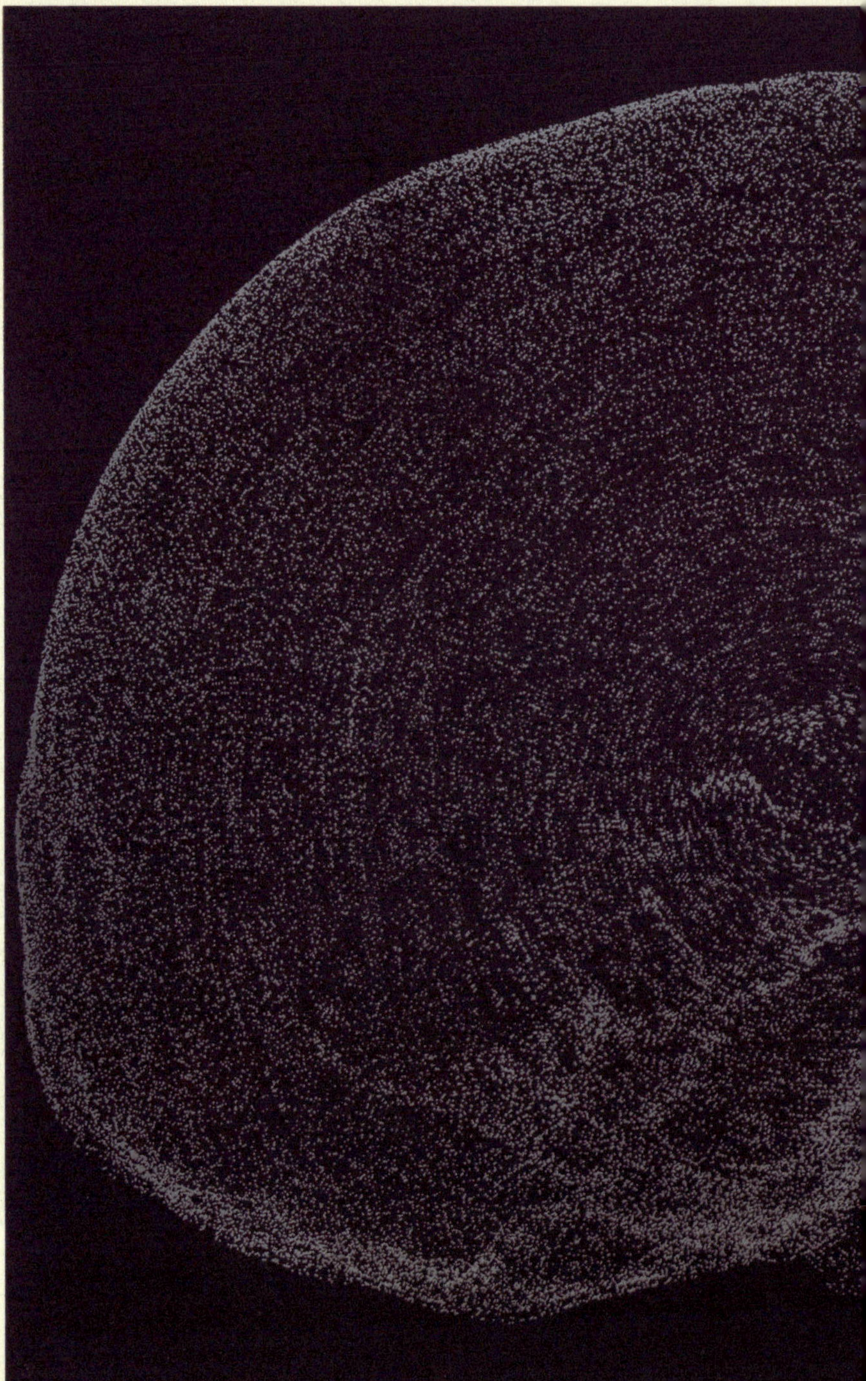

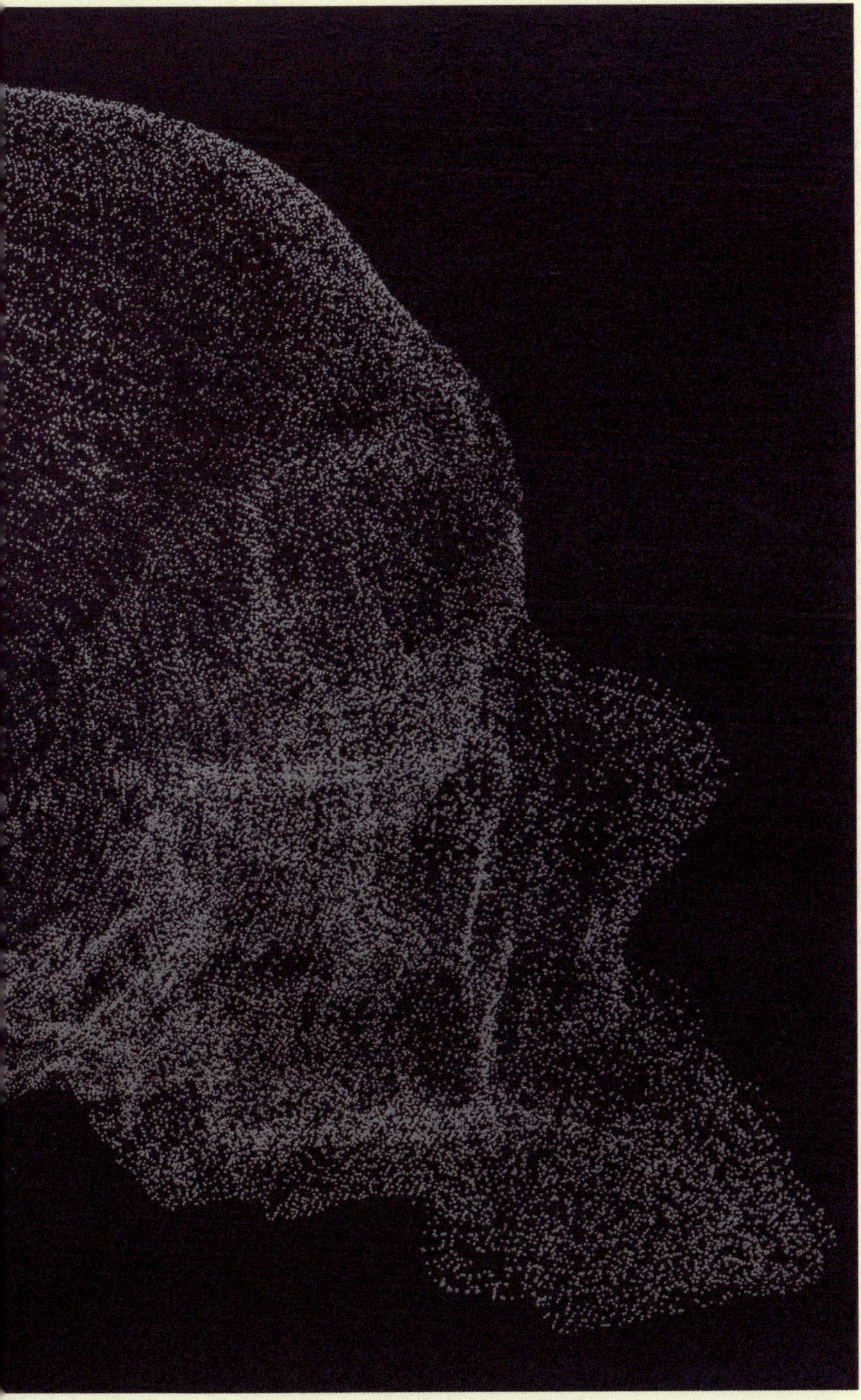

SUPERSIZED

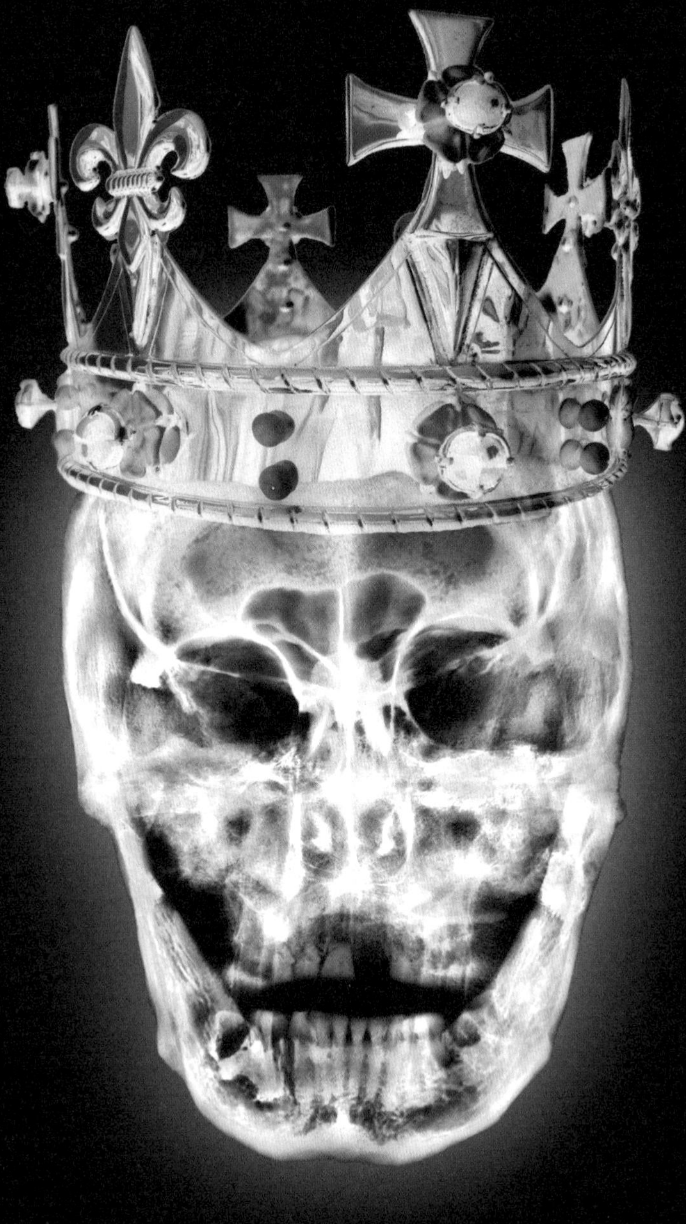

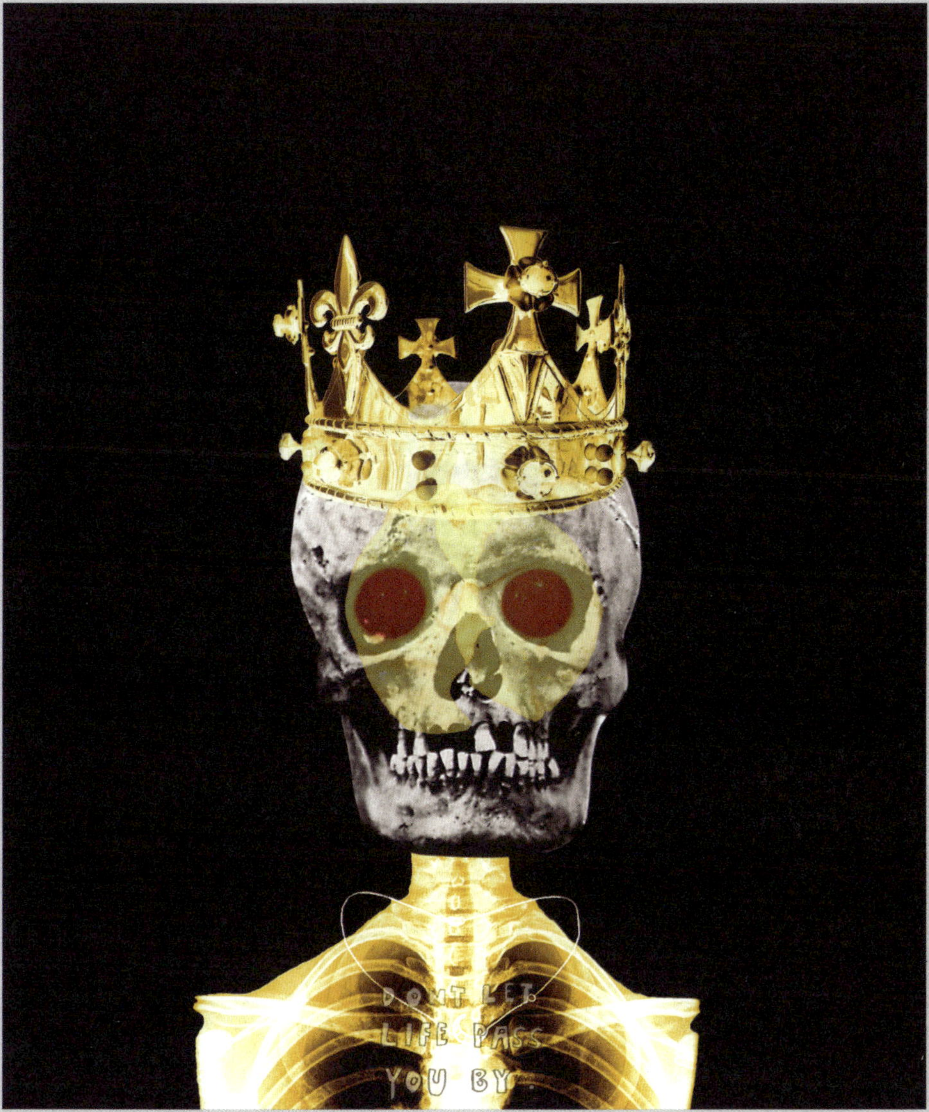
DONT LET
LIFE PASS
YOU BY

The skull provokes an immediate reaction, and its unmistakable contours offer endless possibilities for exploring negative space within a composition. Its rich textural variation also makes it an ideal subject across a wide range of visual contexts.

— ANDIE TAYLOR —

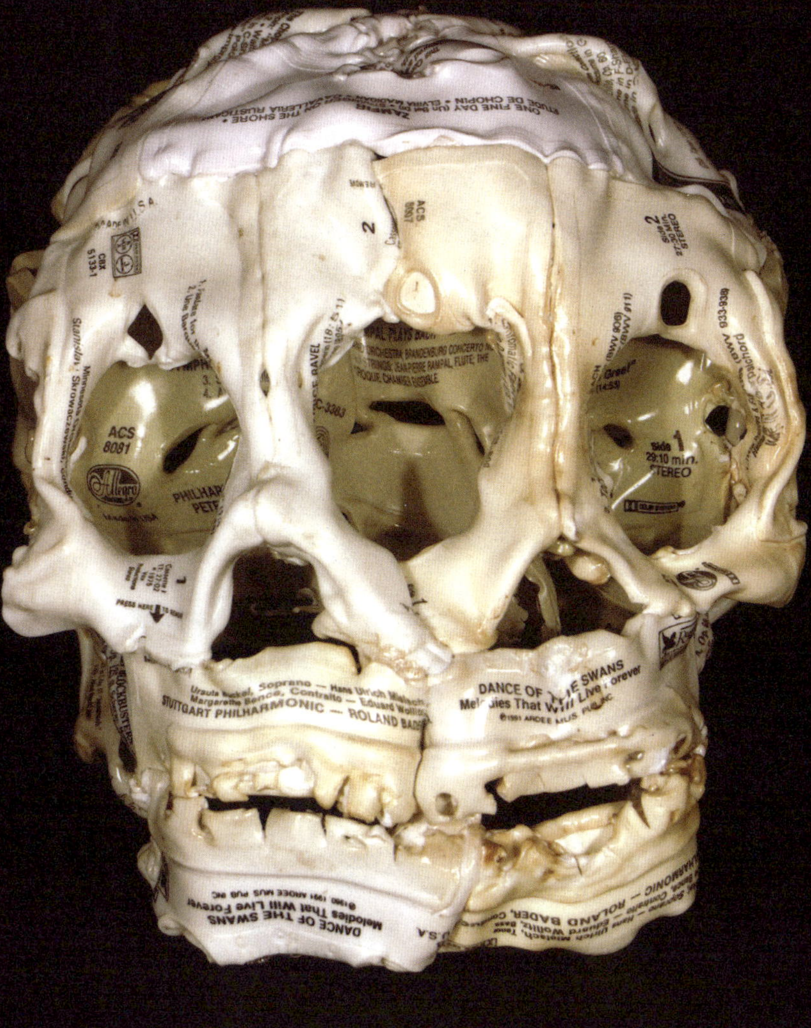
ACS
8081
29:10 min.
STUTTGART PHILHARMONIC
DANCE OF THE SWANS

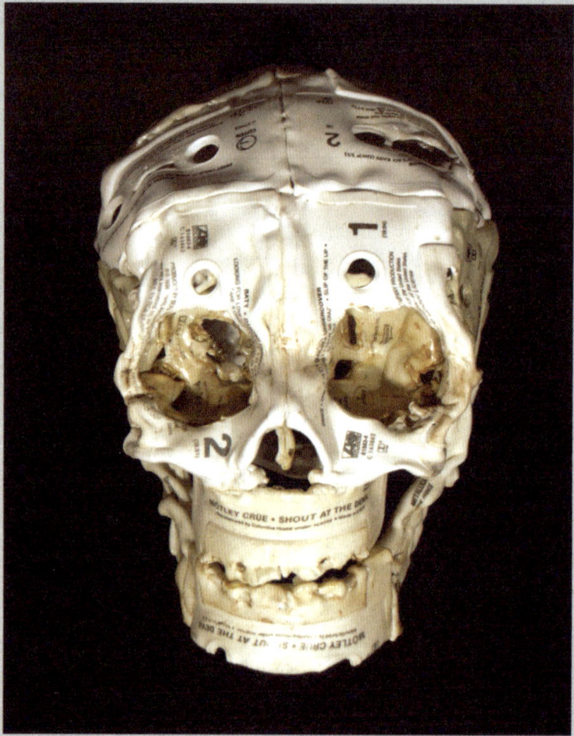
MÖTLEY CRÜE • SHOUT AT THE

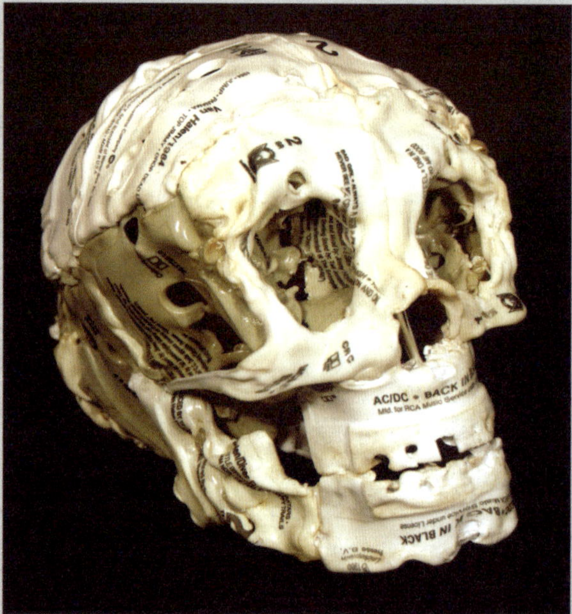
AC/DC • BACK IN
Mfd. for RCA Music Service
IN BLACK

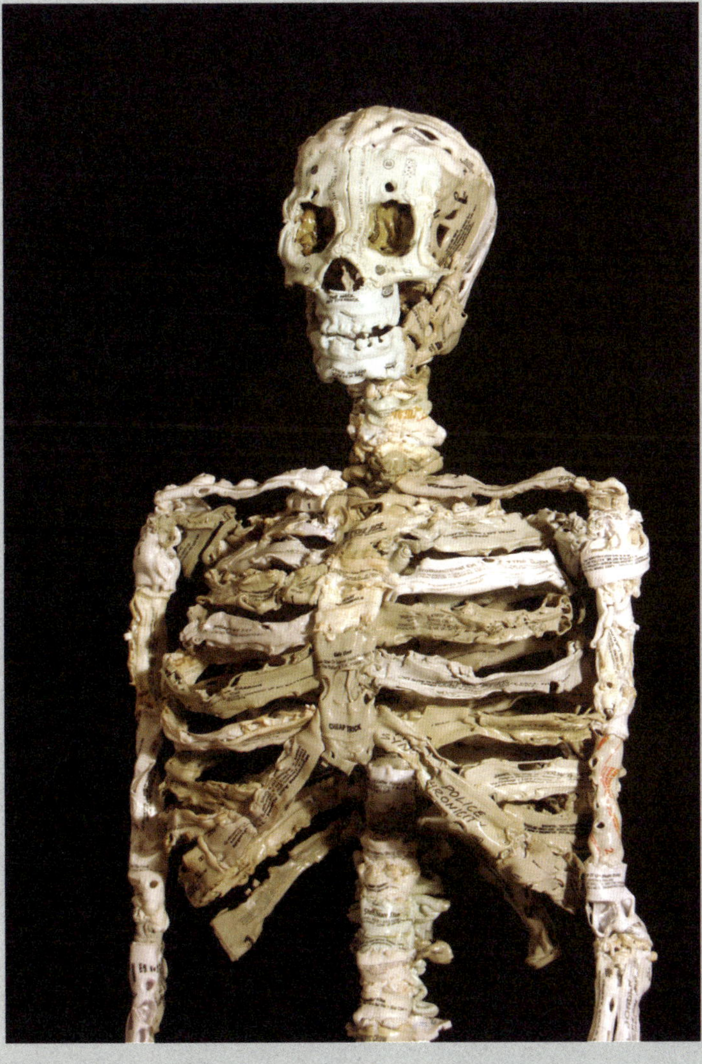

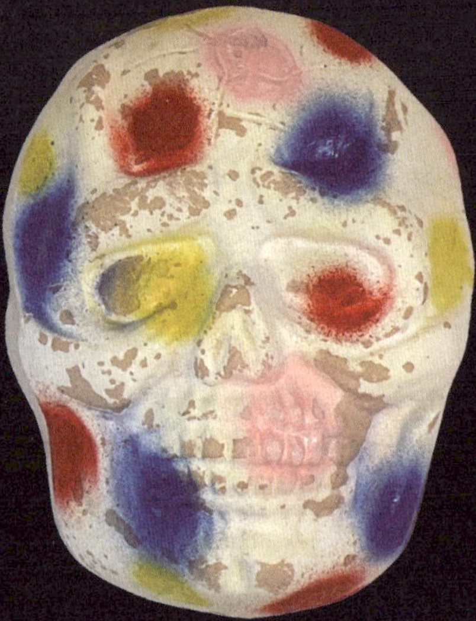

24
AP
S

APS

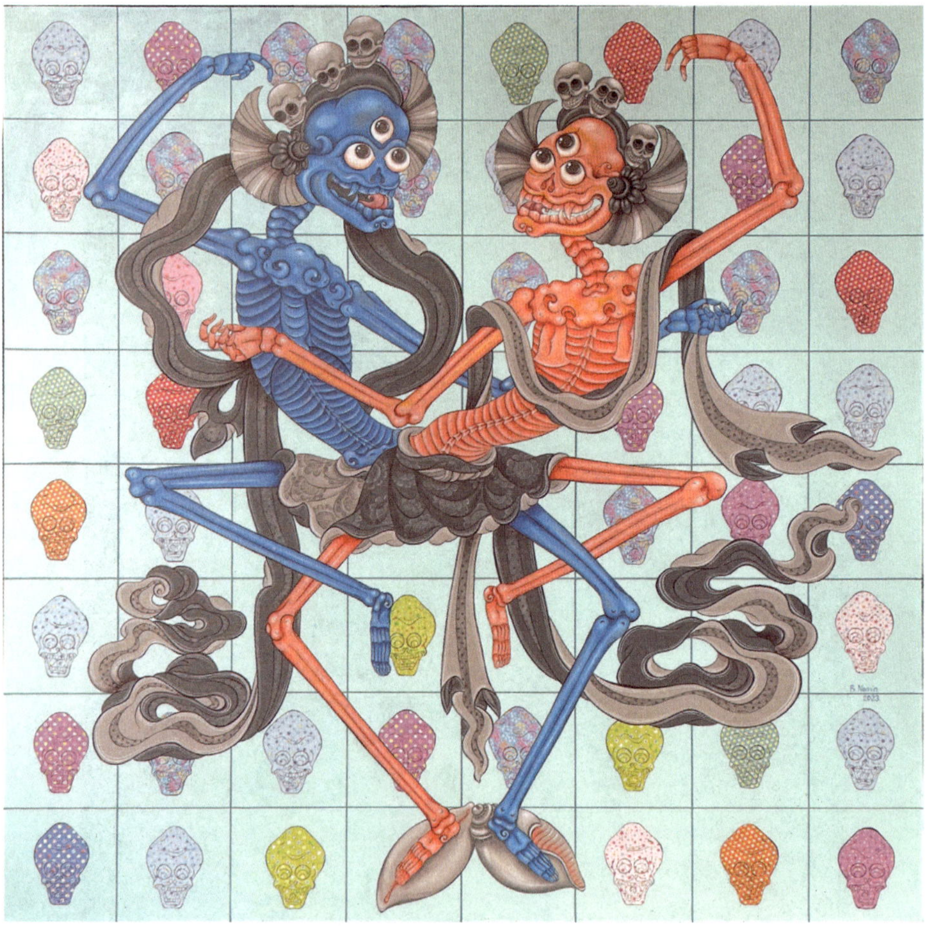

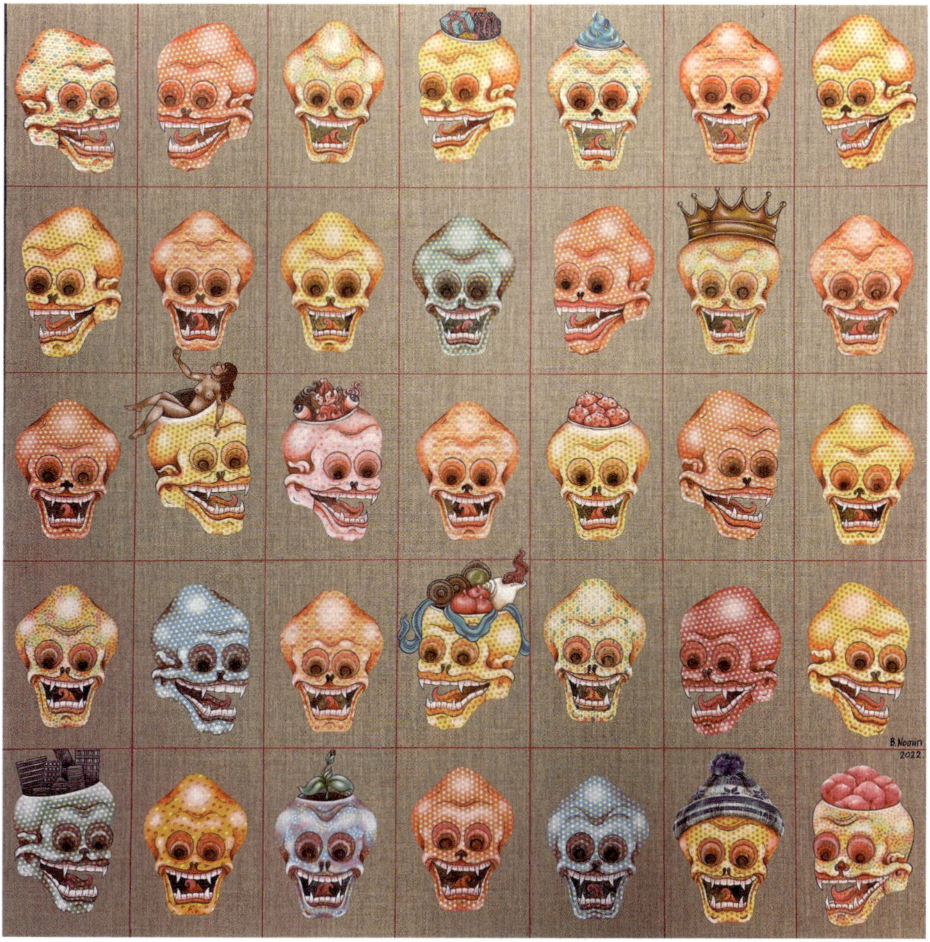
B.Nomin
2022

Beyond serving as a memento mori and a reminder of danger, skulls also embody egalitarianism – their uniform shapes obscure distinctions of skin colour, body type, and background.

— APIP —

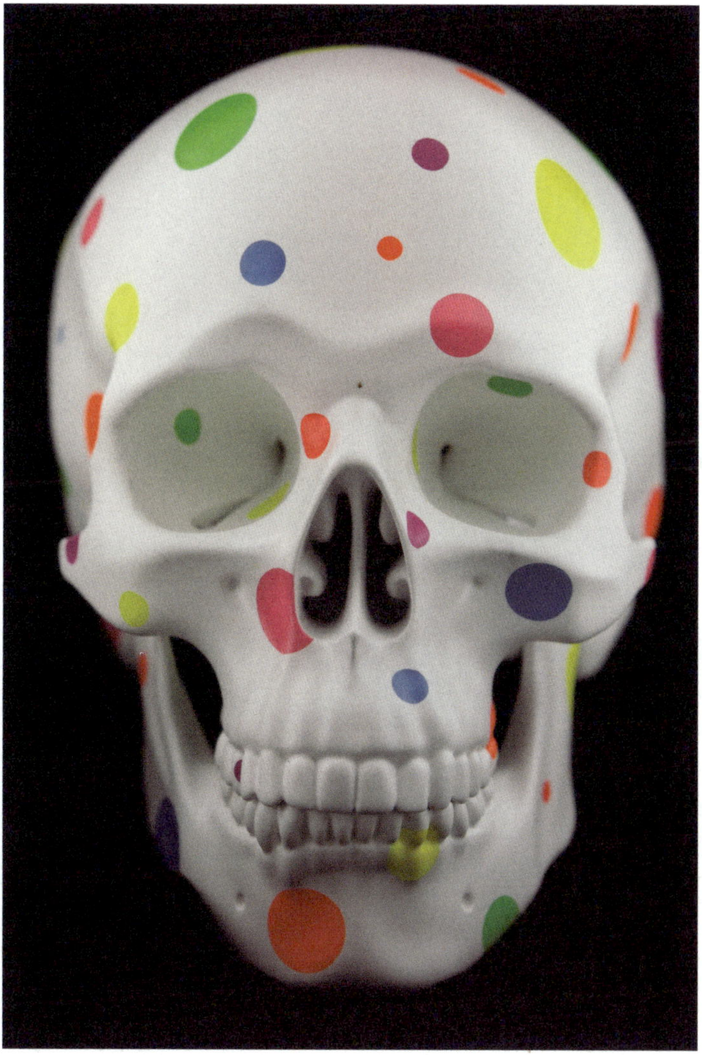

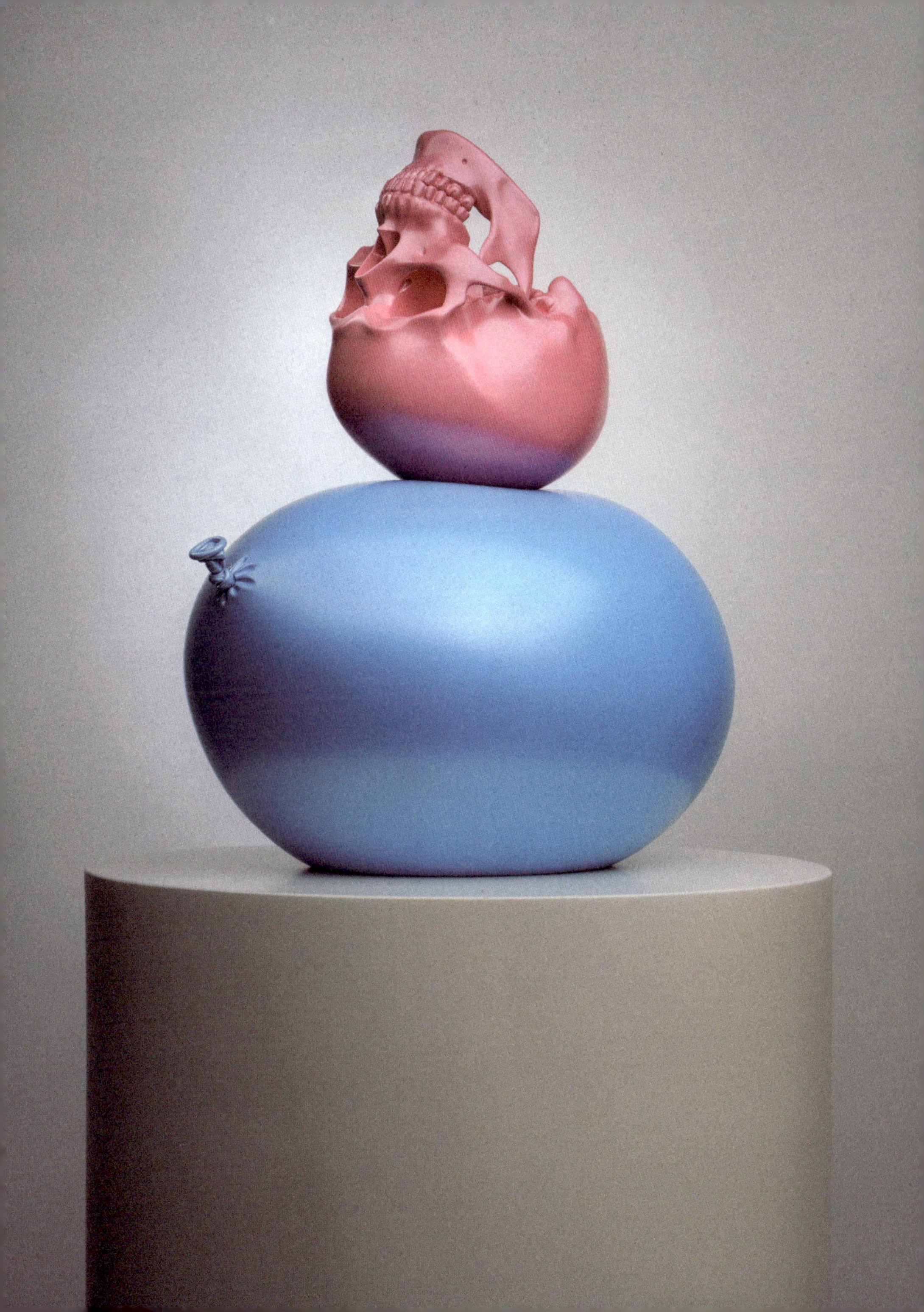

Jim Skull

Our fascination with skulls reflects humanity's paradoxical relationship with death – a mix of fear, curiosity, and a longing for transcendence. As a universal symbol, they embody fragility, rebellion, memory, and creativity across cultures.

– D.VICENTE –

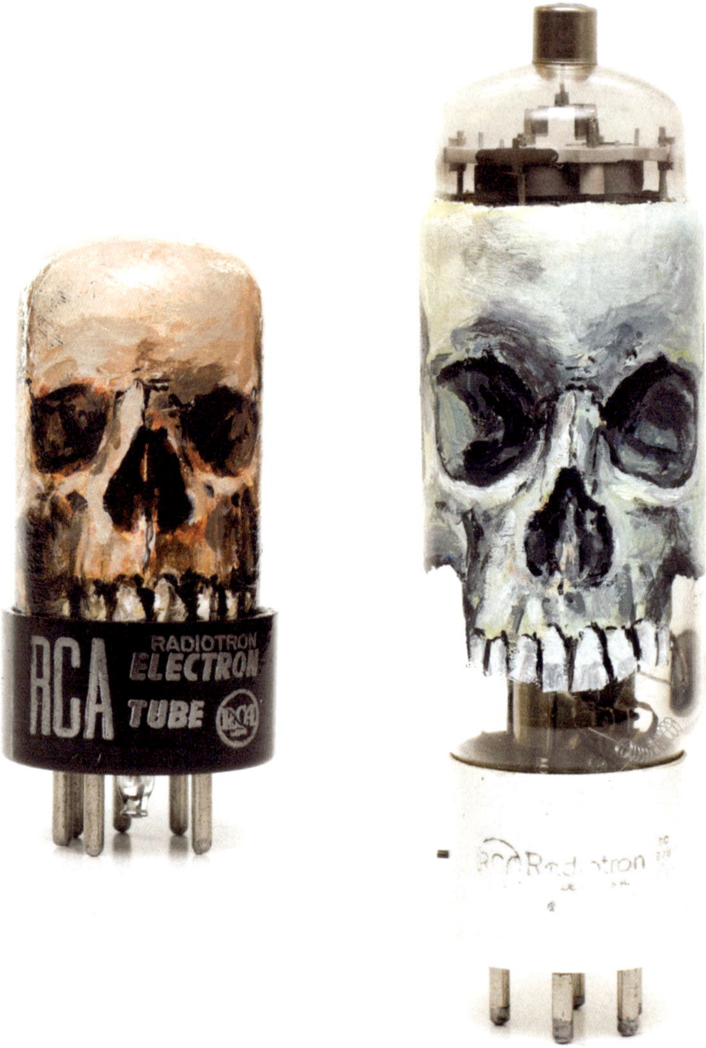
RCA
RADIOTRON
ELECTRON
TUBE

Noah Scalin

SUPER
Super.
STAR WARS
ACTION PACKED
SPLATT
SERGEANT
HONOR
USA ARMY ARMY

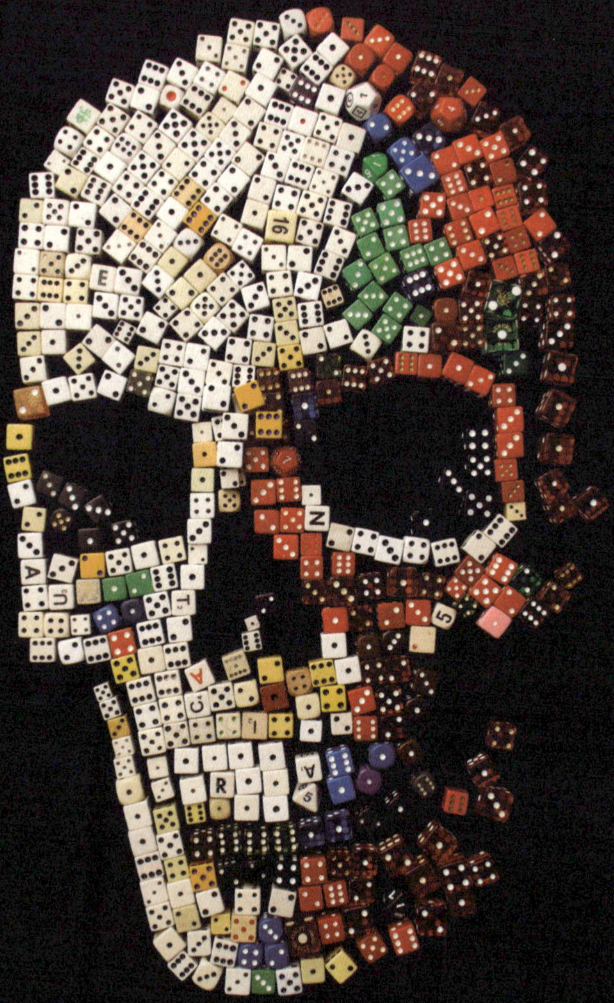

Noah Scalin

Ursus Yogus

Mus Minnius

Homo Ridens

Homo Arnus

Biography

Abed Azarya

Abed Azarya is a Jakarta-based graphic designer, lettering specialist, illustrator, and brand identity designer with over 20 years of experience. His work reflects a deep commitment to craftsmanship, consistency, and the enduring appeal of classic visual traditions.

pp.126-127

Adrien Conrad

Adrien Conrad is a self-taught painter whose punk-romantic style merges fine art and pop culture. A former zombie make-up artist, he experiments with texture to explore a delicate balance between darkness and beauty, as well as death and innocence. Inspired by Rembrandt, Francis Bacon, The Cramps, and The Simpsons, his work blends ornamental detail with an infectious sense of raw, cathartic energy.

pp.162-171, 330

Alexander de Cadenet

Alexander de Cadenet has been creating skull portraits since 1995, using X-ray and conventional photography to reveal a subject's essence beyond surface identity. Each work is titled by archetype rather than name, rendering the sitter unidentifiable and transcending mortality. Over time, his portraits have grown increasingly humorous, reflecting on the cosmic joke of his own approaching mortality.

pp.190, 312-313

Amandine Urruty

Amandine Urruty lives and works in Paris, often from her bed with a suitcase of pens always at hand. Mastering traditional drawing techniques, she creates playful yet deviant portraits that blend grotesque costumes with baroque detail. Her imagery recalls strolling through a Sunday flea market, where second-hand toys and objects carry a duality that is wicked yet peaceful, and decorative yet overwhelming.

pp.226-229

Andie Taylor

Andie Taylor is an Australian oil painter whose work explores philosophical questions of time, memory, belief, and identity. Guided by intuition, his paintings grow as universes of recurring symbols – skulls, scaffolding, rusted cars, birds – forming intuitive,. malleable narratives. Each piece expands from the last, weaving harmony and tension into an ongoing process of self-discovery.

pp.212-217, 314

Andrew Blucha

Based in London for over two decades, Andrew Blucha is the artist behind METAFABLES – a series steeped in the grotesque, surreal, and absurd. Drawing on anatomy, mysticism, and dark humour, his intricate illustrations echo the biting satire of Eastern European art and the influence of masters like Gustave Doré and Roland Topor.

pp.128-135

AP Shrewsbury

AP Shrewsbury is a Michigan-based multimedia artist whose work delves into themes of mortality and transcendence. With over two decades of experience, he has exhibited widely in cities such as New York, Chicago, Los Angeles, and Paris. His recent shows include the Museum of Art and History (California) and the Flint Institute of Arts (Michigan).

pp.318-325

Apip

Apip is an illustrator whose work centres on the expressive potential of lines. Drawing inspiration from scratchboard and engraving techniques, he creates intricate pen-and-ink works that reveal depth and texture through deliberate, rhythmic mark-making.

pp.84-87, 331

Artur Soletskyi

Artur Soletskyi is an artist and educator based in Lviv. A PhD candidate researching alternative art spaces, he works across painting, glass, installation, and video. He has participated in and curated numerous international exhibitions and residencies, with works held in private collections across 18 countries.

pp.230, 250-251

Bart.Woo

Bartosz Wojdyga is a Polish artist and tattooer based in Wrocław. A graduate of the Acadamy of Fine Art in Wrocław. He has been working professionaly in tattooing for eight years. He enjoys merging the aesthetic of engravings and comics, using bold outlines and playful forms to create art that avoids solemnity in favour of irony and mischievous humour.

pp.11-19

Betrayer Family

Founded in 2013 by Surabaya-based artist Anton Wardana, Betrayer Family is a contemporary illustration and lettering studio known for its bold black-and-white aesthetic. Merging intricate illustrations with custom typography, the studio creates designs for apparel, packaging, and branding projects, and has had its works featured in international design publications and art platforms.

pp.58-65

Billelis

Billelis is a digital artist based in Edinburgh, known for his dark yet elegant visual style. His work explores adorned and romantic imagery, developed through continual experimentation and refinement of his craft.

pp.306-311

Brian Dettmer

Brian Dettmer is a contemporary artist renowned for his book sculptures. His work has been exhibited internationally, with pieces held in the Smithsonian American Art Museum, the Art Institute of Chicago, and Yale University. His practice has been widely covered by leading publications and global media.

pp.315-317

Charlie Immer

Charlie Immer is an illustrator known for surreal worlds where playful forms meet macabre themes. His work spans editorial, commercial, and gallery projects, blending humour with dark beauty. Outside the studio, he collects skull-inspired objects and draws inspiration from horror, nature, and video games, exploring transformation and mortality through vivid colours and intricate detailing.

pp.206-211, 257

Chris Piascik

Chris Piascik is an illustrator, lettering artist, and YouTuber known for his humour-driven, energetic drawings that blend punk spirit with cartoon chaos. After 14 years of daily drawings, his colourful, ADHD-fuelled creativity has appeared everywhere from McDonald's packaging to Nike tees – turning his playful art into a global celebration of joy.

pp.89, 106-108

Danilo Brandão

Danilo Brandão is a multidisciplinary creative based in Melbourne, working across art, design, and illustration. With a background in branding and visual communication, he combines clean structure with bold, unexpected visuals, moving between commercial projects and experimental personal work. His practice is hands-on, curious, and rooted in craft.

pp.180-185

Dave Quiggle

Dave Quiggle is a Southern California-based artist whose work blends punk energy, midcentury style, and pop-cultural nostalgia. His illustrations span album covers, posters, and projects for Star Trek and Adventure Time, with exhibitions at Disneyland's WonderGround Gallery and Gallery1988. He is also a recognised tattoo artist at Old Rose Tattoo.

pp.232-237

D.Vicente

David Vicente is a French illustrator whose work channels rock'n'roll, psychobilly, and rebellion. He creates bold, energetic imagery across albums, posters, and skateboards, drawing on 50s–80s American pop culture, B-movies, and comics. His universe features bikers, femme fatales, zombies, and bad boys – capturing a raw, gritty, and cinematic rock spirit.

pp.32-41, 350

Emerald Barkley

Emerald Barkley is a watercolour artist in Northern California. They paint bones and flowers to work through the beauty and devastation of living.

pp.231

Filip Hodas

Filip Hodas is a Prague-based digital artist renowned for 3D renderings that blur reality and fiction. Since his daily render project in 2015, he has collaborated with brands like Adidas, Coca-Cola, and Samsung, and artists including Jean-Michel Jarre. His viral works, such as "Pop Culture Dystopia" and "Lost Data", have been showcased globally.

pp.356-359

Gillian Wilson

Gillian Wilson is an illustrator and screen printer based in Guelph. A BFA graduate from Concordia University, Montréal, she runs her own print studio and produces hand-printed goods. Her graphic style draws on folk art, symbolism, and eerie, unsettling imagery.

pp.92-93, 136-139

Harry Wyld

Harry Wyld is a UK-based artist whose practice spans drawing, painting, print, murals, illustration, and high-fashion collaborations. Blending humour, folklore, and the paranormal, his work captures lived moments with immediacy and clarity. He was named The Guardian's Illustrator of the Year in 2019.

pp.88, 294

Heeey! Design

Heeey! is a freelance graphic designer and illustrator. His bold, limited-colour style draws on traditional tattoo art, punk-rock, and pop culture, often incorporating subtle humour and hidden meanings. He works internationally with brands and bands, creating logos and illustrations that blend wit with visual impact.

pp.222-225, 295

HELLSANDRO

Hellsandro is a mysterious artist, reportedly born in the mid-1980s and currently based in Gorizia. Stories place him across deserts, concerts, and southern Europe, though little is known for certain. His work channels punk energy and irreverent humour, leaving an enigmatic presence that remains alive in both myth and art.

pp.100-105

Hiroyasu Tsuri / TWOONE

Hiroyasu Tsuri or TWOONE is a multidisciplinary artist whose work explores people, places, history, and nature. He creates large-scale murals internationally. Now based in Sant'Elia a Pianisi, his works are held in the National Gallery of Australia, STRAAT Museum, and City of Yarra Collection, and have been exhibited at MUCA Munich.

pp.278-283

Jim Skull

Jim Skull is an artist known for sculptural skulls crafted from fibres, ropes, and natural materials. Since 1980, he has refined a single "perfect skull" form, creating works that balance meticulous craftsmanship with meditative reflection. His practice preserves the skull's mystical essence, offering elegant, introspective alternatives to contemporary pop interpretations.

pp.346-349

Jimi Biscuits

Jimi Biscuits is a UK-based designer and illustrator. His work combines heritage printing techniques, surrealism, as well as minimal shapes and colour palettes, creating a distinctive visual language that channels and distils his ideas through a refined, experimental lens.

pp.66-67, 94-97

Jiri Geller

Jiri Geller is a Finnish sculptor whose meticulously crafted works fuse pop art sensibility with existential themes. Using plastics, metals, and mechanical elements, he creates flawless, machine-like finishes that belie months or years of labour. Exhibited across the world, his art seeks moments of bliss beyond reality.

pp.342-345

Karpichev Artem aka bth3run

Artem Karpichev, also known as bth3run, is a self-taught artist and tattooist based in Tver. Specialising in black-and-white tattoo work, his practice blends precision and emotion through bold contrasts and fluid linework.

pp.90-91

Kate MacDowell

Kate MacDowell creates hand-built porcelain sculptures responding to environmental threats and their consequences. She has exhibited internationally, including at Scope Miami and New York, Art Paris, MOCA North Miami, Urban Nation Museum Berlin, and the Museum of Arts and Design (NY). Her work has appeared in The New York Times Magazine, Hi-Fructose, and Ceramics Monthly, and she has collaborated with a variety of clients such as Erasure, Miike Snow, and HBO.

pp.336-341

Laurina Paperina

Laurina Paperina works across painting, installation, drawing, and animation, reimagining pop culture figures through splatter, mash-up aesthetics, and irony. Her colourful universe borrows from film, comics, and art history, transforming familiar characters with playful irreverence. Her work has been exhibited internationally.

pp.258-263

LIFO

LIFO is a tattooer, painter, and illustrator based in Seoul. Through the lens of Korean identity, he develops a distinct visual language that reflects both a new worldview and a deeply personal sense of purpose.

pp.264-269

Magnus Gjoen

Magnus Gjoen is a London-born contemporary artist whose work merges street and pop aesthetics with fine art traditions. Drawing on history and reinterpreting fragments of the past, he creates striking juxtapositions of beauty and fragility. His work has been held in the Haifa Museum of Art and the Daimler Collection, with collaborations spanning Meissen and the Wallace Collection.

pp.270-275

Manuel Cetina

Manuel Cetina is a Mexican art director and illustrator with over 15 years of experience in vector graphics. Based in Mérida, he creates hypnotic visuals shaped by music, streetwear, and 90s pop culture, drawing inspiration from horror and sci-fi cinema, comics, manga, and anime to craft bizarre characters and retro-inspired worlds.

pp.238-249

Marco Cianfanelli

Marco Cianfanelli is an artist celebrated for large-scale sculptures and public artworks. A graduate of the University of the Witwatersrand, he has exhibited widely and received major awards. His notable works include Release, commemorating Nelson Mandela's capture, and his contribution to The Freedom Park, a national monument to freedom in Pretoria.

pp.276-277

Michael Reeder

Michael Reeder is an urban contemporary artist from Dallas whose work merges graffiti, graphic design, and fine art. Known for vibrant colours, geometric patterns, and figurative imagery exploring identity and mortality, his practice spans murals, canvases, and collaborations with brands such as Santa Cruz Skateboards, New Balance, and Specialized Bicycles. His work has been exhibited internationally.

pp.172-179

Noah Scalin

Noah Scalin is an artist best known for the Webby Award-winning Skull-A-Day project and the League of Space Pirates. His work has been exhibited internationally, including at the Virginia Museum of Fine Arts, Mütter Museum, and Times Square, with commissions for Capital One and Old Navy. He is also the author of six books.

pp.351-355

Nomin Bold

Nomin Bold is a contemporary artist trained in the traditional Mongol Zurag style. Working across painting, installation, drawing, and film, she explores identity, heritage, and modernity. Her work has been shown internationally at Documenta 14, the Asia Pacific Triennial, the Bangkok Art Biennale, and the Havana Biennial.

pp.326-329

Pablo Dalas

Pablo Dalas is a Marseille-based artist and tattooist known for his surreal style, blending comics, folk art, and psychedelia. With over 15 years of practice, his work spans tattoos, murals, ceramics, and pencil sketches, combining diverse mediums with a distinctive approach that delivers imaginative and unexpected pieces.

pp.20-31

Paolo D. Geronimo

Paolo Geronimo is a freelance graphic designer and illustrator based in Manila. His work navigates a whimsical yet eerie visual world, spanning T-shirts, posters, logos, and magazines. With intricate detail and playful wit, he transforms everyday surfaces into imaginative expressions drawn from the esoteric palette of his creative vision.

pp.42-57

Pedro Corrêa

Based in Florianópolis, Pedro Corrêa is a graphic designer and illustrator specialising in packaging, gig posters, advertising, and editorial work. Their clients include The Rolling Stones, Pearl Jam, Queens of the Stone Age, Paul McCartney, Netflix, Dungeons & Dragons, Magic: The Gathering, Cirque du Soleil, and The New York Times.

pp.200-205

Ron English

Ron English is a New York-based painter, street artist, and designer renowned for blending pop iconography with surrealist, political, and consumerist commentary. Known as the Godfather of Street Art, he has exhibited globally, created murals and billboards worldwide, and produced collectible vinyl art figures. His work has been featured in major publications including The New York Times and Art News.

pp.300-305

Scott Partridge

Scott Partridge works across traditional and digital media, creating imagery inspired by the natural world. His work, whether abstract or representational, often features biomorphic shapes and living forms. His influences include Miro, the Surrealists, and natural history illustrators such as John James Audubon and Charley Harper.

pp.332-335

See Machine

See Machine is a multidisciplinary artist whose practice began as a childhood outlet for creativity and coping with anxiety. Trained in graphic design, his bold, flat, symbolic style reflects his design background, while a dark aesthetic – shaped by a fascination with horror, the macabre, and dark art – runs consistently through his work.

pp.111-117

Sinpiggyhead

Nicolas Côme, also known as Sinpiggyhead, is a Paris-based tattoo artist and illustrator. Influenced by 90s pop culture, American comics, and manga, he creates dark yet playful imagery inspired by superheroes, video games, genre films, music, and morbid themes, crafting an alternative universe that blends melancholy with energetic visual storytelling.

pp.72-83

Sophie Donaj

Sophie Donaj is an artist whose work bridges eras, blending contrast and harmony. Drawing inspiration from everyday details, she reinterprets them with humour and irony. Her playful, story-driven visuals invite viewers to look beyond the surface, while her passion for experimentation ensures a continually evolving, dynamic creative practice.

pp.118-125

Stevie Hogan

Stevie Hogan aka Mortar Made is a freelance graphic designer and illustrator. Drawing inspiration from video games and professional wrestling, she creates distinctive illustrations applied across product lines, which she sells through creative e-commerce platforms. Her playful and personal approach informs both his style and commercial projects.

pp.98-99

Stuart Morris

Stuart Morris is a New Zealand-based artist working across painting, printmaking, tattoos, and music. Influenced by German Expressionism and Post-Impressionism, his intuitive, emotive practice draws inspiration from the surrounding world to create work that resonates on an emotional level. He enjoys watching films and gardening.

pp.252-256

Tyler Gross

Tyler is a St. Louis-based freelance illustrator and graphic artist. With an ever-evolving style, his work spans editorial illustration, poster design, and full-service branding, combining versatility with a distinctive visual approach across diverse projects.

pp.140-153

Tyler Spangler

Tyler Spangler is a freelance graphic designer based in Southern California. With a background in psychology and design, he has worked with leading clients including Hermès, Gucci, Nike, Adobe, Starbucks, and The New York Times, creating impactful visual solutions across branding, editorial, and commercial projects.

pp.284-293

Ungfio

Ungfio is a Chilean digital artist whose work explores skeletons and death as universal symbols. Trained at the Catholic University of Chile and influenced by Moebius and Joel-Peter Witkin, she creates raw, sketch-like digital pieces that find haunting beauty in decay, transforming mortality into a striking and relatable aesthetic.

pp.154-161

Valin Mattheis

Valin Mattheis is an artist raised on California's central coast, inspired by an early fascination with bones and the monstrous. Working professionally since 2008, he founded Strange Gods Art in 2011 and later embraced creative writing. Now based in France, he continues to produce paintings, commissions, and concept art full-time.

pp.186-189

Vladimir Chebakov

Vladimir Chebakov is a graphic designer and visual artist based in Prague. Fascinated by the dark and beautiful, he has spent nearly 25 years creating album covers for metal musicians worldwide, working across digital and traditional media. His practice draws inspiration from Central European history and the legacy of past and present masters.

pp.191-199

Vliegwerk Premium

Ruben de Bruin, operating as Vliegwerk Premium since 2015, is a tattoo artist and interior designer known for his intricate blackwork style. His detailed tattoos blend fine lines, shading, and motifs from nature and surrealism, combining engraving-like precision with a distinctive artistic approach that has earned recognition for its complexity and elegance.

pp.68-71

Zero Deluxe

Ben Aldis, known as Zero Deluxe, is a south coast UK-based graphic artist. His career in music, film, and fashion design has evolved into illustration, drawing inspiration from ancient civilisations, exotic wildlife, gothic decorative arts, mid-century design, sci-fi, and psychedelia. He works across printmaking, painting, and other diverse mediums.

pp.218-221

Zhang Ding

Zhang Ding is a Shanghai-based artist working across installation, sculpture, video, and painting, often incorporating live performance. His large-scale, performative projects explore human perception, collective consciousness, and social and political alienation. In 2016, he founded CON TROL CLUB, curating multimedia events that combine subcultural music, visual, and collaborative art experiences.

pp.296-299

ACKNOWLEDGEMENTS

We would like to specially thank all the artists and illustrators who are featured in this book for their significant contribution towards its compilation. We would also like to express our deepest gratitude to our producers for their invaluable advice and assistance throughout this project, as well as the many professionals in the creative industry who were generous with their insights, feedback, and time. To those whose input was not specifically credited or mentioned here, we also truly appreciate your support.

FUTURE EDITIONS

If you wish to participate in viction:ary's future projects and publications, please send your portfolio to: we@victionary.com